50 GREAT TIPS, TRICKS & TECHNIQUES TO CONNECT WITH YOUR TEEN

DEBRA HAPENNY CIAVOLA, PH.D.

New Harbinger Publications, Inc.

Publisher's Note

This publication is designed to provide accurate and authoritative information in regard to the subject matter covered. It is sold with the understanding that the publisher is not engaged in rendering psychological, financial, legal, or other professional services. If expert assistance or counseling is needed, the services of a competent professional should be sought.

Distributed in Canada by Raincoast Books.

Copyright © 2003 by Debra Hapenny Ciavola
          New Harbinger Publications, Inc.
          5674 Shattuck Avenue
          Oakland, CA 94609

Cover design by Amy Shoup
Edited by Carole Honeychurch
Text design by Tracy Marie Carlson

ISBN 1-57224-359-7 Paperback

All Rights Reserved

Printed in the United States of America

New Harbinger Publications' Web site address: www.newharbinger.com

05   04   03

10   9   8   7   6   5   4   3   2   1

First printing

Contents

PART 1

"Whatever": What Your
Teen Is Really Thinking

Enjoy Your Teen

When Jane's oldest child was six months old, she read in one of the parenting magazines, "By now you should be enjoying your baby." Even though Jane loved her child and spent hours smiling and playing with her, she had not thought about *enjoying* the simple pleasure of having this treasure in her life. The teen years are like this, too. You love your teenager, and spend a lot of energy guiding them. Now is the time to delight in the blossoming of this wonderful person you have nurtured for many years.

Your teen is a marvel to watch, exploring their world, testing different roles, and developing a keen sense of humor—even the way their humor falls flat can be a cause of a great deal of laughter. Their room is messy and their music is loud. At times, you may think you're raising an animal rather than a teen!

As wild as this time can be, notice what is great about your teen and tell them every day. You can say, "I love the way you laugh." Or, "You are great at making time for your friends when they need you." As your child discovers their place in the world, you can help them reach their highest potential. Even if your schedule is crammed, find a few moments to take them to lunch, on an errand, or even for a walk with the dog. Discover their hopes and dreams. Stretch their imagination by asking something like, "You really like history. Do you see yourself learning more about the past after you graduate?" They may have no idea what's out there until you link their love of history to working in museums, archeology, or even exploring the family ancestry.

At this point, your teen may not even want to discuss history. They may be concentrating on the path of becoming a rock star. Try not to roll your eyes and chuckle. Go with the flow of the conversation and lead your teen into opening up by reflecting back a few of their words to let them know you understand. "Boy, you've really thought about this. You want to be a rock star and travel around the country." Through your teen's random thinking, you can pick up their fantasies and desires. This sharing draws you closer and gifts you with the enjoyment of celebrating their life. Although today's fascinations may in no way resemble who they will become in the future, their daydreams reveal the many possibilities.

Begin to see your teen's self-discoveries as true wonders. Just as they did as a small baby reaching out, your teen is again mastering the world. Every once in a while, let them be the teacher and you the student. Have them share what they're studying in their classes and express delight that they are learning something new. Decide to focus on what they do well and encourage them to do more. If your teen is kind to a friend who is having difficulty, compliment your child's ability to be a good listener. When they go to the teacher for extra help in a subject, applaud that resourcefulness. Even if your teen doesn't make the position on the team they wish for or a coveted part in the play, acknowledge their bravery in trying when so many others didn't have the courage.

There is such pleasure in watching your teen unfold. Admire their adventures, laugh at their silliness with their friends, or get involved with their excitement as they rush out the door to an event. Your teen is evolving and uncovering their purpose in this life. The process may leave you breathless, but these years will pass quickly as your teen grows, explores, and reveals all they hope for and all they will become. Don't miss out on it.

It's an extraordinary time in your life. To stay deeply connected now and forever, enjoy the wonder of your teen.

The Mystery Within

Taking risks, forgetting to study for a test, or staying on the phone late on a school night; does this sound like your teen?

For years, parents and scientists have blamed teens' risky behavior and lack of judgment on hormones. With greater study and advanced technology, the medical field has discovered that it's not the flux of hormones, but the maturing of the adolescent brain, which must develop further to meet the challenges of adult life. Although your teen's brain is composed of many different sections, the last area of the brain to fully develop is the one that stabilizes emotions and controls the ability to make worthy decisions. This is why you might see your teen having difficulty deciding whether to do homework, call a friend, or go shopping.

Like a computer, your child's hard wiring has to be installed and the software downloaded. This is accomplished through the growth of billions of nerve cells, which increases intelligence, insight, and an awareness of self and others. As your teen moves through adolescence, the quality of their experiences will determine which nerve cells will be cut back and which ones will remain. If your teen becomes involved with sports, school activities, special interests, and academics, they will make choices based on this hard wiring such as going on to graduate school or taking a job in which they are challenged daily. If your teen constantly sits in front of the TV or plays video games for many hours, these cells will be the ones that will decide whether they go on to college, involve themselves in the community, or stay motivated. How your teen interacts with their environment will affect how they behave for rest of their life.

Your teen has the power to determine their own brain development by choosing activities that will stimulate their brain and fine-tune critical thinking. You can help them become the person you both dreamed about by making a conscious effort to create challenging situations for them.

Make a daily, conscious effort to motivate your teen and to show belief in who they are becoming. These positive feelings will help them learn, grow, and retain the nerve cells required for success.

To help your teen train their brain in the right direction, try some of these tips:

- Require them to play one sport or work out at the gym three times a week for forty-five minutes.

- Take them to museums, aquariums, or even to the zoo.

- Watch a foreign film together.

- Play strategic games such as chess or checkers with them.

- Spend a few hours a month at a local bookstore together.

- Enjoy bridge or complex card games.

- Take them to historical landmarks.

Journey to the Center of Your Teen

"Who is this kid?" you might ask as your teen snaps back a testy reply. You may wonder how your child went from crawling happily into your lap for another story to a teen bursting with roller-coaster emotions. Amazingly, your teen is just as confused as you are!

Your teen is rapidly changing both inside and out. Until the age of eleven, your son or daughter had an equal balance of estrogen and testosterone. From the onset of puberty, these ratios change, with a significant increase in testosterone in your son, while it is nearly eliminated in your daughter. In its place, estrogen levels will peak, which means she will cry more easily.

By now you've noticed other changes as well. Your teen's room is probably an image of the chaos they feel. They may have painted their room a funky color, only to want to change it again a few months later. Photos and posters of rock stars, sports heroes, or movie idols are taped on every bit of wall space, and both clean and dirty laundry litter the floor. Your teen will want you to respect this cherished, personal space and can be most unpleasant if anything is moved or tidied. The doors will slam, chores will be forgotten, and music that drives you nuts is turned on when you're trapped in the car. Your food bill will double, you'll find your child sleeping past noon, and you will have trouble separating their ears from your phone. The hours they spend in front of the mirror will not reassure them that everyone in school isn't staring at the large pimple on their chin, and they often feel like a foreigner in their body.

Your teen's classes are more complicated, and soon you may discover you can no longer help with their homework. They worry about bodily changes, take long showers while playing loud music, and think about the opposite sex a lot. Fast food has become a food group and pizza is a staple to be consumed at two in the morning. You never know if you are "in" or "out," but when you're needed it is immediately, if not sooner.

All too quickly, your teen will leave home and the house will be quiet. You can't anticipate everything your teen will encounter, but try to take pleasure in the journey—even when you get "the look." Here are some tips to smooth the way:

- Respect your teen's need for space and privacy.

- Allow their room to be an expression of themselves.

- Set limits on telephone time.

- Be fair, expecting the same from your daughters as your sons.

- Try not to embarrass your teen in front of their friends.

- Take out and share your old Beatles and Monkees records.

- Tell funny stories of when you were a teen.

A Day in the Life of Your Teen

Take a look at the day of sixteen-year-old Lauren.

6:20—I look blearily at the alarm clock. Another day of the same old junk.

6:25—Into the bathroom. This is my time, I think about everything in the shower from what I'm going to wear to what people have said to me the day before. I think about the homework I will have to do at lunch because I was too tired to do it last night. So don't bother me while I'm in here. Besides, I can't hear you over my CD anyway.

7:00—I stand in front of my closet, finally deciding what to wear after fifteen minutes of staring at my clothes. Then, on to makeup. Honestly, I hate makeup. Who knows why we put it on? I guess I just feel more confident with it.

7:40—Great. After the forty minutes of grueling preparation, I'm going to be late.

7:50—I make it to school with just enough time to go to my locker and meet up with Courtney before we go to French. Courtney looks mad this morning. She tells me why, and I tell her she has every reason to be.

9:05—Third period, Chemistry. Oh no. I left my sweatshirt in my locker. I hope the teacher won't give me detention. If I just sit down, then I'm safe. Okay, I made it. Stupid midriff-baring rules. We do problems on the white board. I talk to my friends Kevin and Ashley the whole time. My poor lab partner feels left out.

10:30—Math class. I swear I have some of the weirdest teachers. We sit there and laugh at his pea green shoes and his 1..2..3 Hats off!! It's the greatest.

11:20—I wait for Mandy, and we complain about everything.

11:25—I don't want to go to band. About a week, and the season is over. I can't wait until I get my Fridays and Saturdays back. Good. I get to stay in the band room today. Well, not so good. My friend Bryan and I got into a fight. I won, of course.

1:05—History. I hate this class sooo much. While we watched the movie *Glory,* I talk to my friends. Christine and I flirt with Rob and make him blush.

2:00—This teacher seriously hates our class. Charles and I think she's a big partier because she is such a mess every day. The class is so much fun. I get nothing done in this one. My teacher gets so mad at us. My planner is filled with really weird hangman games, and my book cover has a bunch of random stuff written all over it. I was sitting next to Charles because (surprise, surprise) he doesn't have his book. We are supposed to be reading, but we sit and talk the whole time. Finally, the bell rings.

3:15—Band practice. It was long, and we had to run for talking, which we might have gotten away with if the cymbals hadn't crashed. It takes another twenty minutes after practice to get everything down the hill and back into the band room.

6:00—I finally get home and eat dinner. I start my homework, and an hour later Dave calls. We talk for about twenty minutes and then get back to our *huge* piles of homework. I finish at 10:00 and then have to get ready for bed.

The alarm clock ringing makes me start my repetitive life all over again. I personally think it wrong that anyone should have to wake up to an alarm. Thought for the day: Have you ever noticed that power outages always happen during the day so you can always reset your alarm clock, but never during the night? I think it's a conspiracy.

Learn the Signals

All teens at one time or another will indulge in behaviors that are a cause for concern. Most of these unsettling behaviors are temporary, lasting only a few days or as long as a week. If they go on longer, keep the lines of communication open so your teen will feel more comfortable coming to you if they need help.

Jennifer was fifteen when her mom and dad began to notice she was spending most of her evenings after school in her room. She would come down to eat but would only pick at her food, even when her favorite meals were prepared. Her friends called, but Jennifer preferred to stay home, playing the same music over and over again. One day after Jennifer had left for school, her mom decided to clean up her room hoping to find a clue to her change in behavior. As her mom straightened up, she noticed a note tucked between a few of Jennifer's favorite CDs. It said, "Life stinks. I don't care what happens."

Many parents believe their child's room is private, but if you're worried about your teen, all bets are off. Your first responsibility is to your teen's well-being, and this may mean monitoring their personal space. Most of your teen's behaviors are not a cause for concern, though you still want to check where they've been on the Internet or with whom they've been hanging out. Review what they've been watching on TV or at the movies, as well as what they are reading or listening to.

Since emotions are stored in the body, a primary key to understanding your teen's inner thoughts can be their body language. Look at your teen's shoulders, where they cast their eyes, and how they walk up the stairs. A person's posture represents their physical space and is the mirror image of what is going on inside.

Start with the expectation that your teen is well, but needs more sleep or more balance in their life. If your teen continues to wave the red flags of isolation and easy frustration after they've had more rest, be vigilant. Look for changes in behavior and find a quiet time to talk with them about your concerns. Always keep a reservoir of hope that the alarm bells you hear aren't really signals, but a need for closeness and connection.

The following behaviors may seem odd at first, but really can be considered "wellness signals":

- Your teen spends the majority of their time in their room, on the phone, or listening to music.

- They have a voracious appetite for fast food, sometimes skipping meals at home.

- They sleep until noon after staying up late the night before.

- They have mood swings, with a direct correlation between lack of sleep and low frustration tolerance.

- They debate and challenge your decisions with increasing problem-solving skills.

If your teen exhibits more than three of these "concern signals," seek professional help:

- A weight gain or loss of ten pounds or more

- Difficulty falling asleep or sleeping too much

- Rapid changes in mood that occur daily

- Isolation from friends and family

- A drop in two or more grades in one semester

Tap into Your Teen's Sense of Fairness

"It's not fair!" your teen yells as they slam the door to their bedroom. You just finished explaining why they can't stay out past the set curfew to go to the after-prom parties. "Everyone else's parents are going to let them do it!" they yell from their room.

Even as a small child, your teen had a strong sense of what was fair and just. "Mom, Jim got a bigger piece of cake than me." "Alice got to be on the team, and she doesn't even come to practice." This sense comes from an inborn awareness of the difference between needs and desires. There is a difference between "I need to be heard," and "I want new sneakers." Yet, it's still important to look beneath your teen's outcry of what is fair. When your teen declares, "Everyone else can stay out to midnight," their underlying message may be, "I need to have a later curfew so I can be included in this group of friends."

The hallmark of fairness is predictability. Are you consistent in your expectations and your requests for behavior in similar circumstances? Inconsistency confuses your teen's sense of fairness and is a powerful reinforcer encouraging them to push until they get what they want. However, it's important to remember that being fair does not necessarily mean being equal. Not every child in your home will have the same bedtime or even have the same driving privileges.

Your teen needs to know that what is being asked of them is being asked of others as well. Begin by having your entire family come together to decide what will be considered fair in your home. Describe your challenge in trying to keep your expectations equal, and offer a few suggestions that will bring peace to your home, such as having the same house rules followed by everyone.

By nature, we are drawn to what is fair and honest. A sense of fairness can be a way of gauging the world through the lens of what is right and wrong. To be fair is to be unbiased and honest. One teen said to his father, "Listen to me, Dad. I just want to tell you my side. After all, you make me listen to you when you want to tell me something." His dad thought about it for a few days and then broached the subject with his son. "I was thinking about what you said the other day, Peter. I make you listen to me, but I don't always listen to you, and that's not fair. I'll work on that." Maintaining fairness creates security and respect in your relationship without permitting your teen to jockey for power. It also has a warm and compassionate lightness that leads to your teen feeling better understood.

Use these points to check your level of fairness:

- Do you see the other side?

- Are your rules and reactions predictable?

- Do you make your teen listen to you without listening to them?

- Are you consistent?

- Is each issue of unfairness addressed and dealt with justly?

Through fairness, you offer a safe environment for your teen and an example against which your teen can measure their behavior. More importantly, your fairness lets them know that they can count on you to uphold what is just and fair.

Shrink the Influence of Unhealthy Friends

Mary overheard her son, Dylan, say to his friend on the telephone, "It's going to be a great party. None of the parents will be home. When do you want me to pick you up?" Inwardly, Mary shuddered from fear that her son was getting into trouble. It seemed, each month, Dylan was moving further away from her values, beliefs, and expectations and more toward his friends' way of life. Mary steeled herself for the confrontation and entered his room.

Your teen's friendships are essential for a number of reasons. They assist in forming your teen's identity, set the stage to learn how to set limits and boundaries with others, and teach respect and compassion, as well as emotional intimacy. You may find that you're a little nervous about the importance your teen places on these relationships because you're afraid that their friends may persuade your child to shirk responsibility, get in trouble, and cause conflict at home. However, their interactions with friends serve as a bridge from playing ball in the park to the game of interpersonal communication in adult relationships at home, at work, and in all social situations.

Your teen has best friends, close friends, and acquaintances. They will also be a member of a crowd or even several crowds of teens from an assortment of different cliques. Belonging to a crowd is essential to your teen's well-being and impacts whether they feel accepted or rejected by their peers.

You can make a difference. A strong connection with you is ten times more powerful than the influence of your teen's friends. The more secure your child's attachment to you, the more they will respond well to others. When your teen believes you care about them and are committed to remaining connected, they will be less likely to become involved in behaviors that would distress you.

To shrink the influence of bad friendships, develop a good relationship with your teen by making sure you are never too busy to talk. Ask them what classes they enjoy and who they talk to between classes. Their answers will give you insight into their life and the people they are attracted to as friends. Make your home a place friends want to hang out by having space, snacks, and entertainment available. Develop relationships with the parents of your teen's friends. They can be instrumental in helping you create parity in the rules your teen experiences in both homes, so there is less conflict and more agreement. Expand your teen's circle of friends by including some of your own adult friends or members of your extended family in their activities. Some of the most successful teens have parents' friends in their lives to laugh and share memories with and who care about what happens to them.

Remind your teen of times they've thought independently and remained true to their own values regardless of friends' choices. Teach them how to better read their friends' reactions by recognizing facial expressions and encourage your teen to smile more, especially when setting limits with friends. Be clear about what you believe in and reward compassion and consideration.

Stretch Your Teen's Wings without Ruining the Furniture

Sherry was certain she wanted to be a veterinarian when she grew up. She had raised many pets including snakes, turtles, guinea pigs, mice, birds, cats, and dogs. Her father called their vet and asked if there was any possibility Sherry could spend a day with him at work. After spending eight hours tending to animals, she decided she wanted to pursue a career in the medical field. With her father's help, Sherry examined and revised her junior- and senior-year courses to include more sciences and math. She joined Future Doctors of America and took a part-time job at a nursing home. Sherry was gaining the experience and course work to achieve her dream.

Ideally, beginning in freshman year, small steps toward your teen's aspirations can be taken, but it is never too late to evaluate what your teen needs to achieve to go on to college or enter the career of their choice. Ask your teen to describe their perfect job and how it would contribute to their happiness. Include questions such as "How many hours a week would you like to work?" or "How much income do you want to make?" Tell your story of why you changed jobs or careers, or even what you would have done differently if you could do it over again. Weave into the discussion how you learned to set goals and the commitment it took to achieve them.

Helping your teen choose classes wisely for their junior and senior years can be fun. Based on the knowledge you both have gained from discussions about their goals, review their options. Explore together the requirements necessary to enter their career of choice. You can do this through talking to others in the profession, searching on the Internet, or researching in the library. Perhaps your teen has decided to forgo college and attend a trade school. What are the prerequisites for entering? Whether college or trade school, your teen will need to select challenging high-school courses that will enhance their ability to further their education.

As your teen approaches junior year, help them explore whether they'd like to go to school locally or out of state. Have them think about the size of school they would like to attend and the advantages of each. What do these colleges require for an SAT or ACT score? To show colleges your teen is serious, make sure they continue to take challenging classes all through senior year and show leadership in the community through extracurricular activities or volunteer work.

The time you spend with your teen learning about different occupations, colleges, and classes will enrich your relationship. By creating an interest in common, you can explore career opportunities together and work as a team rather than feeling like you need to push your opinion. This will also help your teen become more invested in the process and makes an easier transition from high school to their future college or career.

Here are some tips to get you started:

- Create a life plan with short- and long-term goals.

- Have your teen take some of the free career-assessment tests on the Internet.

- Sign them up to take an SAT prep course and use preparatory software or tutoring.

- Explore financial aid and scholarships by junior year.

- Visit at least three colleges, if feasible.

- Set up internships or volunteer opportunities to explore different occupations.

Look before You Love

Your teen is facing the exciting and probably daunting world of dating for the first time. Recognizing people who will add to their life requires you to maintain an ongoing dialogue to offer insight and understanding. You can connect with your teen by revealing the basics of effective, fun dating, helping them gain mastery over this essential skill.

Dating is a healthy social competence that develops confidence and intimacy. You can prepare your teen to date by encouraging them to build a friendship with someone first and to recognize the difference between a crush and love. How does your teen know if the hottie is a player? Years ago, teenagers would date, become involved, and then break up. Today, teens are hooking up without even dating. By getting to really know that hottie, your teen can discover whether the friendship could or should become a romance.

A great way to begin learning the basic dynamics of dating is to first develop friendships with the opposite sex by hanging out with groups. This helps your teen learn how to open conversations without the pressure of impressing or becoming a chameleon. Your teen can follow this with dating in a group setting, then proceed to double-dating, then to one-on-one.

Perhaps you are concerned that your teen is telling themselves that they aren't as good as the person they want to date. Emily calmly told her mother, "A guy asked me out today. I don't think you'll like him." With a steady voice, her mom asked, "Why?" "Well, he has a motorcycle, has piercings, and has lots of girlfriends." Pausing, Emily's mom looked directly into her daughter's eyes. "Oh Emily, is that all you think you're worth?" Let your teen know that they will attract healthy dating relationships when they feel good about themselves and are enjoying their life.

Empower your teen through awareness of the principals of dating, such as the importance of going out with different people to discover their own needs and wants in a relationship or dating someone because they like them as a person, not because it makes them more popular. Anticipate considerable discomfort as you go on to explain what behaviors are acceptable on a first date: whether there should be kissing or touching, where they should go, how long the date should last, and what to do when pressured. Also, remind them that whatever they do on a date will most likely become public teen knowledge.

How do you know when your teen is old enough to date? There are three primary criteria: they should have friendships with the opposite sex and be able to maintain reasonable boundaries with them; they've gone in groups of greater than three to a variety of activities over the past year; and they know how to get out of a bad situation.

Let your teen know the best dates are ones where they can be themselves and are free of stress with plenty of laughter. When your teen is happy with life, they are a magnet to others who love their life as well.

Here are some fun things to do on a date:

- Play with the animals in a pet store.
- Roast marshmallows on a barbeque.
- Go to a park and play Frisbee golf.
- Take photos in a booth.
- Go down a giant slide.
- Launch a model rocket.

Shape a Sense of Self

Your teen needs your help to develop the strong sense of self necessary to have the courage to be successful, build good relationships, and enjoy the abundance already present in their life. Self-esteem changes and develops over time and is emotional nutrition that feeds your teen's soul. It's never too late to help your teen build strong self-esteem.

There will naturally be times when your teen will not feel good about themselves. Perhaps this occurs when they're left out of a party, ignored in the hall by a good friend, or have no date for the dance. How your teen views themselves physically will also impact their level of self-esteem. Amanda begged all summer to start plucking her eyebrows. She was absolutely certain that she would look like the class sweetheart, Liz, if she could just change this one little thing. Amanda excitedly lay down on the couch as her mother plucked, anxiously awaiting her transformation. When her mother was through, Amanda leaped to her feet and excitedly stared in the mirror. She was devastated. She could not even tell! Amanda burst into tears.

By remembering back to your preoccupation with how others viewed you and your insecure feelings when you were a teen, you can teach your teen to de-emphasize the importance of appearance and focus more on developing their personality. Help your teen strike a balance between their achievements and an appreciation of their top qualities. You can do this by consciously applauding their positive efforts, regardless of results, always being careful not to lay it on too thick: "Lexi, no matter how boring the subject, you are still able to write an interesting report."

Empower your teen to be who they truly are and to set boundaries around relationships that are unhealthy. Grant your teen the courage to confront and ask for what they need, and the strength to walk away. Kristin was great when she and her best friend Hallie were alone, but at school Kristin teased Hallie. After discussing the situation with her mom, Hallie told Kristin that she would no longer drive her to school until she apologized and quit talking "trash" about her. Her mother was pleased that her daughter was standing up for herself.

To shape your teen's sense of self, give at least one compliment, no matter how minor, every day. Instead of waiting for a holiday, use your good dishes or light candles to show your teen's importance to you. Initiate dinner discussions about people who changed thoughts, attitudes, and beliefs, people like Franklin Delano Roosevelt and Martin Luther King, Jr. Let them know how important it is to forgive themselves when they make a mistake and that a disappointment does not mean failure. Show how to turn a weakness into a strength and how to connect with others through empathy and compassion.

Here are some steps your teen can take to create a strong self:

- Recognizing that accepting one's self and becoming happy is a choice

- Forgiving themselves and learning from past mistakes

- Asking directly for what they need

- Writing in a journal about their feelings

- Enjoying successes by making a list of what they do well

PART 2

What Does Your Teen Believe In?

Inspire a Belief in a Higher Power

There is a force beyond ourselves that we can move within or push against. Many of us who have teens today grew up in the "me" generation, where authority was something to be resisted and controlling our own lives was considered a virtue. Our beliefs put the burden of our survival and well-being completely on us. It can be a lonely and empty world when the only person you truly depend on is you. Although it may require a change in our thinking, let's do something different for our teens and inspire a belief in something greater than their selves.

Believing in a higher power can elevate your teen to do extraordinary deeds. This belief can give meaning to your teen's life and nurture a respect for authority. A societal conscience is created, so they can look outside themselves to realize how they belong to the world and how they can make it better. It will help heal their heart and teach them how to let go and forgive. Your teen's burdens will be lighter as they learn what they can hold on to and what they can change.

Your teen will face life challenges with the belief that someone is watching over them. As an athlete, they may see a connection between their belief in a higher power and their ability to do well on the playing field. Or, as a student, they may experience a link between prayer and gathering internal resources to do better than anticipated on a test or project.

No matter where your teen is on the spectrum, you can still encourage them to call upon this higher power when needed. First, let your teen know this higher power is always available to them; this interconnection will give them courage. Open the door to prayer by establishing an observance at dinner or in the evening before bed. Speak from your heart and use words that acknowledge help from above. Explain how numerous prayers will be answered in ways they never dreamed possible and that some will not be realized in the way your teen planned.

Model respectfulness to authority by having your teen honor his elders with an emphasis on teachers, police, and other people in the community who go out of their way to help others. Let your teen know that even if you do not believe they are necessarily right in all matters, you respect their decisions and the positions they hold.

To lift your teen to greater spirituality, hope, and courage, offer them a sense of expectancy that there is something that is uniquely theirs to accomplish here on earth. One young teen asked, "Mom, what do you think my purpose is? Why do you think I'm here?" He and his mother explored contributing in a meaningful way to the lives of others and how he could begin today to shape this honorable undertaking.

Spirituality is a commitment. Do not claim to know all the answers, but let your teen know how this belief has held you up in your times of need. Give concrete examples where a weight was lifted, bringing you peace and resolution. Talk about the miracles that have occurred in your life or the lives of others you have known well. At the dinner table, discuss the connection between healing and spirituality and how faith is not something that can be seen or touched.

Your teen's multifaceted gifts and talents go beyond genetic accidents and given abilities. The mystery of a higher power can help explain this personal uniqueness to your teen, which assists in making life-altering choices and sculpts their life. Inspire your teen to believe in something greater, so they can listen for who they are and know that their life has a purpose.

Encourage a Life of Balance

In our "hurry-up" society, the pressure to do more in less time is filtering down to our teens. Although stress can be good for productivity, it can also be overwhelming as the intensity increases for teens to excel in school, join activities, volunteer, help out at home, and have a part-time job. By following these tips, you can detect if your teen is burned out and create a stronger connection through your commitment to conceive strategies that encourage a life of balance.

Most likely you're wondering how much activity is too much and what is too little. The answer lies in the balance of your teen's daily living habits and routines. Your teen requires a minimum of nine hours of sleep at night to be rested. With studying for tests, chatting on the telephone or the Internet, or playing video games, your teen may not be getting the rest they need. This leaves them sleepy for early morning classes and interferes with their memory. If your teen's grades are not as high as you would like, first take a look at their sleeping habits.

A pattern of nutritious eating is also essential to your teen's well-being. Often the entire family's lifestyle does not support regular meal times or lots of home-cooked meals. Even with schedules tight, you and your teen can sit down once a week and make a list of healthy snacks, juices, and foods that they can eat on the run. Include grains, vegetables, fruits, and dairy with enough protein to support skeletal and muscle growth. If your teen is watching the pounds, help them manage their time so they can work out or wake up early enough to have breakfast before school. Also, no caffeine or sugar after seven in the evening.

Ensure that their school schedule and after-school activities allow them to stay motivated without overinvolvement. Today, to participate in sports, events, or clubs demands an enormous amount of time, possibly leaving your teen exhausted and mentally drained. But even if your teen is busy at school, they can still maintain a healthy life style with a ten-hour work week. Having a job develops a good work ethic and leads to accountability for managing time and money. It's also important for the work to be meaningful without becoming so consuming that it interferes with school responsibilities. Encourage them to save 50 percent of all they earn.

Although their life may seem in disarray, there are many things that are within your teen's control. Assist them in identifying unhealthy patterns and focus on one at a time that will dramatically improve their life. Make a conscious effort to stand by your teen, not over them, as they attempt to make these changes. The more your teen is personally invested, the greater the chance that these new modifications will stick, their stress will diminish, and balance will be restored.

To encourage a life of balance, try these suggestions:

- Establish regular sleep rituals and schedules.

- Ask your teen to identify what they could do differently to eat better.

- Put "downtime" into daily routine.

- Make changes gradually; pick only one per week.

- Ask what they can do for themselves or someone else that day.

- Bust stress by laughing, making lists, and choosing optimistic friends.

Promote Moral Responsibility

Are you worried about the state of the world in which your teen is growing up? Do you wonder how you can raise a child of character?

In the real world, character counts. It grows from a belief in moral responsibility and connects your teen to family, community, state, country, and world. Moral issues challenge your teen every day. Does your teen cut in line to get lunch or allow others to get in front of them when they are in a rush? Do they indulge in white lies or tell the truth and take the consequences? Do they stand by or stop the bullying or teasing of another teen? Moral responsibility is more about your teen's way of thinking than the ability to make good decisions.

Take a careful look at your own actions in your daily life. Do you put the shopping cart away at the supermarket, so it doesn't damage another car? If the cashier makes a mistake, do you go back and give them the correct change? The big things are easy and obvious. But it is how you act each day that speaks volumes to your teen.

Remind your teen about character. After they spend the weekend at a friend's home say, "Tell me how you showed good character." You will be amazed how your teen will become aware of the times they revealed these qualities. Show how honesty pays off by introducing them to successful and ethical business people. You can also have your teen spend time with grandparents or other elderly people who are willing to share their wisdom and experiences in the face of challenging situations.

Tell stories about moral conflicts to your teen and ask how the dilemma could have been solved without giving your position on the issue first. Give examples of everyday concerns and ask questions about the consequences of people's actions. Work through your teen's struggles with deciding what is the right thing to do. When your teen has not shown moral responsibility, ask questions about the outcome. "How do you believe your behavior affected them? How do you think they felt? What could you have done differently?" Then explore together what your teen could do to repair the damage.

Model what you expect, keep promises, and regard others on their merits. Promote fairness, moral integrity, and relationships based on honesty. Discuss the difference between lying and standing up for what your teen believes is true, and show courage when other parents challenge you on your efforts.

Here are the cause-and-effect relationships between your behavior and your teen's responses. Remember, you're the model for your teen's behavior:

- When you keep promises and do what you say you will do, your teen sees reliability and honesty.

- When you have the courage to do the right thing, your teen feels trust in and respect for you.

- Staying steadfast in your tolerance of differences, you model acceptance.

- By being accountable for your choices, you demonstrate strength.

- When you show compassion to teens and those less fortunate, your teen sees caring.

- When you are quick to forgive, your teen hears compassion.

- By obeying laws and rules, you model citizenship.

Discussions on moral issues in everyday life need to occur all the time, not just in special moments. Become your teen's moral consultant and nurture compassion for all people. Promote moral responsibility because our teens are the soul of our nation.

Find the Missing Peace

A long time ago, there were two parents, Amy and Donna. Amy wanted more than anything for her teenage daughter to be popular and someone she could be proud of. When her daughter's grades started dropping and she began to skip school, Amy became angry and distraught, worried about what everyone would think of her as a parent.

Donna worked long hours, but looked forward to spending the evenings with her family. Her kids were not always polite and the house was often chaotic, but Donna was happy. One day, Donna's son came home and with a snarl and shot out the words, "What's for dinner?" Donna turned and asked, "Are you alright?" Her son snapped back, "Yeah." Later that night, Donna went into her son's room and sat on the edge of the bed. "Bad day, huh?" Her son quietly nodded.

Amy looked for happiness outside herself and became resentful when her teen refused to make her mom happy. Donna found happiness within rather than looking to her teen. Because Donna was responsible for her own happiness and peace, she was able to offer unconditional love and hear the feelings behind the words.

To bring peace to your home, make a conscious decision to create harmony within yourself rather than placing the burden upon your teen. A peaceful home evolves through a slow and steady process of seeing and "hearing" your teen with new eyes, creating an emotional experience that changes old beliefs and conditioning involving the learning of new attitudes and behavior. Your happiness cannot depend on whether your teen is happy or sad, grumpy or mad. It is internal. You can model this for your teen as well.

You can restore peace to your family by doing something different than you have done before. If your teen gets loud, is irritable, or debates, say, "I can't hear you when you speak to me like that." When your teen is disrespectful, calmly look into their eyes and say, "In this family, we speak nicely to one another." Being clear about acceptable behavior teaches your teen they can control their emotions.

How you think about your teen will also create your reality. Even though you may make every effort to not show negative thoughts in your physical attitude, you can't fool your teen. Their sharpened radar tells them you are quiet on the outside, but angry on the inside.

To become more peaceful, step outside your thoughts and watch the pattern of your "stinkin-thinkin" (how you take one problem and magnify it into a bigger one). As you begin to think about your teen, do you feel rising tension? You usually become aware of this feeling in your chest or stomach. By recognizing your physical reaction, you can become aware when you start with a pleasant thought and snowball it into one that creates an unhappy mood. To stop yourself, exhale without taking a big breath and think about something frivolous with no emotionality attached, like how you would spend lottery winnings.

If you are restful inside, your teen will not disturb your inner peace. A peaceful home is likely to yield a peaceful teen. Here are some tips to increase the peace:

- Think about a peaceful period and what worked at that time.

- Look closely at your conditioned responses, the way you react to your teen's behavior.

- Focus on your teen's words rather than what you are feeling.

- Give your teen (especially boys) a language that describes feelings.

Be a Light in the Darkness

There will be times in your teen's life that their world seems shadowed by impossibilities, crisis, and loss. When encountering these turning points, your teen may not know how to ask for help. Be your teen's light in the darkness. Lead them forward to tomorrow's hope through your love and compassion.

The loss they experience may be from a close friend moving away or not making the team they tried so hard to earn a place on. Moreover, a crisis may arrive when they fail a test or lose a friend to illness. James's best friend had a heart too big for his chest. Derek had surgery the year before and seemed like he was finally well. One afternoon, while he and James played basketball, Derek's heart unexpectedly stopped. In that instant, James was propelled into despair. He struggled with reconciling how his sixteen-year-old friend had died so suddenly. Through his parents' loving support, and hours of talking, James began recovering from the pain.

Through times like this, your teen will struggle to make sense of their world. Hope that life will be better may seem elusive. Lift their spirits by becoming an anchor. Share a few of your stories of overcoming adversity to demonstrate how you changed your world for the better. Recount what you first thought, your feelings, and your mood. Describe the process of recovery, including how others helped you and what they did to lift your pain so you could begin to heal. Leave your teen with a lesson of how you gained strength to go on and how it altered your view forever.

What you do makes a difference. Your teen may feel as though something precious has been lost, but by instilling a belief that tomorrow will be better, you offer your teen an unequivocal way out of hopelessness. This renews their mental energy, so they can go on to find new pathways when the old ones are blocked. This is how they'll learn resiliency and understand that they have the power to surpass their expectations.

Let them know that life is good and the difficulties they encounter will only bring a deeper and richer meaning to their existence. Teach them how to positively talk to themselves internally (self-talk) to succeed and overcome obstacles. Use words like "challenges," "chances," and "opportunities." Be a confidant and a friend and gift them with your warmth and comfort when they feel no one understands.

If you strive to be your teen's support, your relationship will never be the same. Through your expression of unconditional love, acceptance, and positive regard, you will have brought it to a higher level, greater than you ever dreamed possible. Despite any disagreements in the past, you are there to listen, care, and offer light in the adolescent darkness.

Here are some phrases you can use that offer hope:

■ "Things are turning around."

■ "You're moving in the right direction."

■ "You have the hang of it."

■ "Tomorrow you will feel better."

Eight Healing Words

There are words and concepts you can use within your family that promote healing and strength to face another day. These words connect parents and teens so their relationships continue to flourish, becoming closer, more loving, and life enhancing.

Forgive. To forgive means to give up, let go, and move beyond the hurt. Forgiveness is a personal healing process that clears the path to make room for good feelings. Teach your teen that by holding on to past hurts, they give their power and energy to another person. Ruminating over thoughtless acts stops them from recognizing the wonderful offerings in their life. Forgiveness brings the peace to focus again on those things that will enlarge their life. Demonstrate forgiveness toward your teen so that they can open their heart to trust again.

Trust. To bring your relationship with your teen to its highest potential, establish a mutual trust. Give confidence to your teen that your expectations and actions are consistent. Trust will help make the worry and fear of your child's adolescent years minimal, as you believe your teen will choose to do the right thing the majority of the time. Trust opens both of your hearts to risk believing that others keep their promises.

Thank you. Your teen craves to hear that what they have done is meaningful and worthwhile. This feedback needs to come directly from you. It tells them that you are pleased about the choices they've made. A spoken "thank you" shows gratitude for the contribution your teen has made to you and to the family. It is a warm habit that will form a lifetime of thankfulness.

Appreciate. By showing appreciation to your teen, you are offering unconditional love and positive regard. It creates a sense of security and certain belonging to your family.

You're also letting them know that they are worthwhile and an important person. To appreciate is to let your teen know you recognize their value to this world.

Sorry. To say this word with sincerity makes deep healing possible. It shows responsibility for your actions and a willingness to turn a wrong into a right. You will deeply connect with your teen when you are able to look them in the eye and apologize for a mistake. It tells them you are not always right and that it's okay to admit an error. Through "sorry," they will understand the importance of being vulnerable to help another let go of hurt.

Tomorrow. As a teen, all that happens seems immediate and forever—what happens today predicts the next day. Give hope that tomorrow will be better. The word "tomorrow" offers insight and acknowledgment that there may be a difficult moment, but that moment will pass and, overall, life is good.

Respect. Respecting is acknowledging that your teen is not a reflection of you, but an individual who is unique. In raising a teen, you acknowledge that it isn't the differences that matter, but how the differences are handled. A search for middle ground is a high priority when both points of view are respected.

Courage. To persevere despite all odds is the message you send by being courageous. It will give your teen confidence to get up again, even if they've fallen too many times to count. No matter the striving to separate, with courage you will always remain your teen's hero.

Establish the Groundwork for Gratitude

With high-school parking lots filled with shiny new mustangs, BMWs, and parents' hand-me-down Lexuses, how do you nurture gratitude in your teen?

Your teen may truly believe they need a nice car to be accepted or the latest haircut to be noticed. A great deal of this thinking may be based on what our world tells them they should have. Because of their developmental phase, you may not be able to create a totally grateful teen at this time, but you can begin to establish the groundwork for gratitude.

Gratitude is appreciation in disguise. Your teen is not born with the ability to recognize a situation as valuable or give thanks unless they know what to be thankful for. When they thank you for attending their activity, say, "You're welcome. It means a lot to me to hear you say that." Compliment them when they share: "I know it was difficult to let your sister wear your dress to the party. Thank you, that was really nice." Being grateful is a skill learned through your reinforcement of values. Your teen will absorb values not so much by what you say, but by how you live and what you expect of them.

To connect your teen to feelings of gratefulness, listen to their concerns and pressure to be like everyone else. Develop strategies to delay gratification that make it easier for your teen to resist the urge to buy. For instance, they can keep a notebook of all the things they want. Several weeks later, your teen can look at this list and realize how many of these same things are no longer important to them at all.

Share your beliefs about what gratitude looks like. Describe in real ways why it's important to acknowledge the good and how it will affect their happiness. By doing your own gratefulness homework you can give your teen an idea of what appreciation looks and sounds like. Point out ways you are grateful in your everyday life. "Wasn't that great of Dad to fix your shelf even though he's so busy?" "How nice of Mr. Hart to change my tire."

You can also show appreciation for your teen's behavior. Express thanks for helping with housework or just for being such a great kid. One parent thanked her son for how he handled himself when she gave him a consequence for a speeding ticket. The next time he misbehaved and there were some angry words between them, her teen thought about it. He came back a while later to say, "I'm sorry I raised my voice to you, Mom." Some understanding of the value of their relationship had taken root.

Arrange natural opportunities for your teen to practice thoughtfulness and to express gratitude. Have them consistently write thank-you notes or call grandparents after receiving a gift. They can also buy birthday presents out of their own money or flowers for a sick neighbor. Copy gratitude sayings and periodically put them around the house. Place them on the refrigerator, as a screen saver, or even in your teen's pocket. These notes of appreciation can also be tucked under their pillow. "Your room looks great. Thanks for making my job easier."

Living a life of gratitude presents your teen with a lifetime of caring and allows them to recognize the miracles in life. It shows them just how beautiful life can be, even in the simple daily acts of living.

Overcoming Obstacle Illusions

How is your teen's temperament different than your own? Does it interfere with how you relate or get along? Perhaps you enjoy the quiet in your home after a long day, while your teen craves the stimulation of having friends over to watch movies. You might think before you speak, while your teen expresses every thought they have in their head. You file every piece of paper, while your teen can't locate their English book.

How you interact with and see your teen largely depends on the differences of distinctive personality traits. Once you understand the contrasts, you will better be able to influence how you perceive and act toward your teen.

Their actions may seem the direct opposite of what you want and expect. These differences can set up parents and teens for considerable miscommunication. If you speak in bullets, your teen may hear commands and control. If your teen avoids eye contact and pauses before they speak, you may perceive this as them being untruthful. If you're very talkative while your teen only has two close friends and spends little time on the phone, you may be worried that they're depressed rather than simply introverted.

Explore your own personality style. Are you a "driver" personality who wants things done your way without dialogue or input? Or are you more amiable, acquiescing rather than risking conflict? Do you trust your gut when making a decision, or are you methodical, researching out the details? Are you uncomfortable with surprises, or do you value spontaneity?

Comparing and understanding how you can communicate according to your teen's style can help make it easier for them to connect with you in life-enhancing ways.

Friendly. The friendly personality type is agreeable, respectful, and willing. They think well of others, are sensitive and quickly hurt, embarrass easily, and fear confrontation.

Talkative. The talkative personality enjoys being with people, is highly verbal, and speaks before thinking. They are emotional decision-makers who are dramatic and often disorganized.

Logical. The logical personality is a creature of habit. Highly organized, they think internally before speaking. Slow decision makers, they are uncomfortable with surprises.

Driver. The driver personality is time conscious, strong willed, and an independent risk taker. With direct, bulletlike speech, they make statements more than ask questions.

If your child is a friendly personality type, be relaxed and moderately paced when interacting. Be sure to avoid harshness in your voice and draw out their opinions. When your teen is talkative, adopt this fun-loving behavior, discover their dreams, and tap into their competitive spirit. Because you know your talkative teen's internal time clock is broken, you can grant more flexibility than structure.

Your logical teen requires you to be more moderately paced and needs your permission to proceed deliberately and slowly when explaining ideas. If they are indecisive, encourage them to make a decision even if all the facts are not in. Overstatements and exaggerations turn them off, so be exact and factual when providing details. Your driver teen needs you to be on time, fast paced, and stay on topic. Focus on results, be organized, and ask rather than tell if you need them to do something.

You know your teen well. Look for clues to how your approach to communication is similar or different. Neither one of you will make dramatic changes in your personality style, but you can significantly influence how you relate to one another by finding middle ground to make it easier for you to connect.

Love the Unlovely

Just when teenagers need their parents to love them the most, they inevitably are trying their hardest to push them away. From ages thirteen to eighteen, adolescents are not always at their best. One moment they love everyone; the next they have "no friends." They are prone to let all those within shouting distance know what they're feeling and get annoyed easily, especially at parents, siblings, and even the family dog! Many parents, half in truth and half laughing, say they cannot wait until their teen graduates and leaves home.

Even though it's difficult not to take the rejection personally or react negatively to the sound of a whine, this is the time to love your unlovely teen the most. When your teen is cranky, radiate warmth, understanding, and kindness, and strive to separate the behavior from the person. In your mind, say, "I am unhappy when they act disagreeable" rather than, "They are so irritable." How you frame your teen's behavior will significantly impact your ability to stay connected in the rough times. How you portray the unlovely behavior to your other children and spouse will influence how they interact with your teen, too.

Your absolute acceptance of your teen is the foundation for unconditional love. Let them know that despite their unbecoming behavior, you love them anyway. You may think your teen knows this already at some level, but they regularly worry that you couldn't possibly love them as you once did. No matter what the level of distance or irritability, your teen still has a deep desire to know you love them just as they are. By letting them know that you still believe they're special, your teen can work through those unlovely times more quickly without consequences to their esteem and who they believe themselves to be.

These are the moments when it is meaningful to say, "I love you," without the expectation of hearing it back. Hold in your heart that your love for your teen is not dependent on whether they exhibit love toward you. Knowing the love you feel for your teen is enough. Over time, your teen will respond consistently to your message of positive regard and will flourish under your unconditional love.

Here are some tricks to help you love the unlovely:

- Tell your teen "I love you" at least twice a day.

- Every other week, write a one-sentence note about what you love in your teen. Surprise them by leaving the note in different places, such as on their pillow, bathroom mirror, or car.

- Offer unconditional love even when it's not reciprocated.

- Ask "How can I love my child more?"

Connection Quotient

Colin went to his grandparents' home near the beach for several weeks one summer. He jumped off piers into the ocean, waded in small tide pools looking for hermit crabs, and spent every hour with cousins, aunts, and uncles. Colin soon realized he had many people who cared about him and believed he was a great kid. That fall when Colin returned to high school, he was just a bit more confident, needing the approval of his friends just a little less. Colin knew he belonged to a much greater circle of those who loved and believed in him.

The most challenging job you'll face in their adolescence is to help your teen understand that a happy and successful life is built upon a process of connection. One of the best ways to keep the thread strong is to link your teen to their extended family, helping your teen believe that they are truly important to a large group of people who care about their life and future. It's up to you as the parent to keep these relationships going. It requires effort to keep these attachments strong, and the message of "family first" will help your teen appreciate that their family life cannot be replaced by friends.

Perhaps your teen lives a long distance from the extended family. Keep connected through weekly telephone calls, letters, and pictures. Discover creative ways to get together. If you can't all go visit, allow your teen to go alone. Your extended family will come to know your teen in another light without you present, and your teen will more securely attach to these family members, relying on them to meet needs while away from home.

If there has been distance between you and your family, this might be a great opportunity to reconnect and bring your teen into the circle. The close ties they develop with the extended family will give them a sense of belonging to something greater. These constant relationships over time with family members will influence your teen's social interactions and develop their self-confidence in relating to a variety of people.

Besides connecting with extended family, find new ways to feel close to your teen. During dinner or when driving in a car, tell your teen about the day they were born or how excited you were to learn you were going to have a child. Talk about your years of growing up and the loving relationships you developed within your family. Perhaps you had a cherished bond with a grandmother or an uncle. Have a discussion about how your family has helped you through your more difficult times and has been there when you needed a hand. Let your teen know that they, too, can access this family support.

Because of our extended family, we feel a greater sense of belonging to the world we live in. Each person is interconnected to create an unbroken whole. It is our obligation to keep these links intact to the very best of our abilities.

PART 3

How Does Your Teen Really Feel?

Take the "P" out of Power Struggles

Chris was finally going to a long-awaited concert one hour away in the city. He was taking four other friends who had arrived minutes before and were eager to go. Instead of insisting he arrive home by curfew, his mom took out a piece of paper. On it, she estimated when the concert would end and calculated how long it would take to drive each of the friends home. Together, Chris and his mom set a time that was realistic. It would have been easier to say an emphatic "No—you need to be in by midnight. Leave the concert early." But, more than likely Chris would be absorbed in the music, forget to watch the time, and end up leaving late and missing his curfew.

Power struggles can become mutual efforts that allow your teen to become a separate individual while you guide them toward success. Just as your teen is discovering how to be independent, you too will be challenged to learn new skills to navigate this unexplored territory.

You may engage in debates out of fear and anxiety as you watch them make mistakes. You may try to save your teen from tough decisions by telling them what to choose, how to choose, and with whom to choose it. This sets you up for conflict and some serious head butting. Much of what happens between you and your teen you can control. Step back and watch how you give instructions. Remember, you're communicating as much with your tone and body language as with the words you choose. Do you ask questions or tell? Do you force an issue or do you try to understand their reasoning?

What worked to resolve power struggles in their childhood often loses its effectiveness. Teen years require a new way of thinking. Is your teen ready to make good decisions independently? Certainly not! But they believe they are, and there lies the challenge. As your teen progresses toward forming a separate identity, they have a driving internal need to protest, debate, and negotiate. Negotiating does not imply you're giving in or even attempting to compromise. It means creating a win-win situation for both you and your teen. When there is a true learning experience, both of you walk away satisfied.

To stay out of daily power struggles, create a biyearly behavioral contract. Begin by outlining each expectation from homework to chores. Be specific and make sure 75 percent of the contract is negotiable. Sit down with your teen and discuss each item. Let them work with you to decide the level of expectation as well as the consequences for failing to abide by the rules. This may seem like a time-consuming process, but the contract will eliminate daily conflict and help preserve the quality of your relationship.

Here are some guidelines to creating a contract with your teen:

- Create a new contract each summer and fall.

- Negotiate 75 percent to increase your teen's personal investment.

- Debate the small stuff so your teen feels more powerful and in control.

- Have your teen decide the consequences for a broken contract.

- Both you and your teen sign and date the contract, each keeping a copy.

When You Ask Questions and Get Bad News

You wait, mouth dropped open, wondering what to say next. Taking a breath, you hold it, struggling to sit until you hear the *whole* story. You stayed up until your teen returned from a date. Innocently, you asked, "How was your evening?" Sitting down next to you, your teen said quietly, "I went to a party, and it was raided."

This is not the time for a strong reaction, no matter how your gut is wrenching. Your teen's willingness to come to you when in trouble comes from the mutual trust and respect you have built up over time. Let your teen know it's safe to tell you and that you really do want to hear the news. Be judicious in your tone of voice and easy in your body language. By spontaneously coming to you with bad news, your teen is asking for your support and understanding.

Try not to look shocked; keep your face relaxed and without much expression. Nod your head and reflect back a few words to persuade your teen to continue, and try to let them finish before you ask questions. Probe until you fully comprehend the problem and let your teen correct any misconceptions. Then ask, "What part do you own in this?" If your teen begins to backpedal, use encouraging, open statements like "And what happened next?"

There may be times when you know you should ask a question, but you're not ready to hear the answer or act on it. At the moment your teen is presenting bad news, it's important to first listen with compassion. The discipline can come later, after you have had time to mull over the incident. Let your teen know that there will be consequences, but they'll be less severe because they've told the truth.

If you find yourself reacting badly to the news, maintain eye contact and make a conscious decision to keep your composure. Try not to be afraid of what your teen is telling you and begin to interrupt or change the subject. By responding to the incidentals you may find yourself going in the wrong direction and causing your teen to clam up.

Within every problem lies a solution. Your mission at this point is not to rescue but to offer hope that together you can find a way to turn the situation around. In faith, your teen has come to you, trusting you will understand. You know you have built a strong connection when you ask questions and you get bad news.

Here are some techniques to help you receive bad news more effectively:

- Sit at same level, so one of you isn't towering over the other.

- Display the attitude you can handle whatever your teen will say.

- Look directly into their eyes when talking, and keep a relaxed, attentive posture, nodding your head and avoiding fidgeting or looking away.

- Reflect back the message and let your teen correct any misconception.

- Use open-ended statements like "Can you tell me more about that?"

- Offer advice only after your teen has exhausted what they want to say.

In general you can use these tips to build trust with your teen:

- Act rather than react.

- Work together to create solutions.

- Praise efforts to come talk to you.

- Take time to connect each day.

Know When to Challenge, Probe, or Support

Ryan's friend Shep was failing his history class. When the grades for a recent test were being passed out, Shep became excited when he saw Ryan had an "A." He leaned forward and whispered, "Great! I copied your test. This will bring my grade up." When the teacher gave Shep his test back it was marked with a big red "F." Confused, Shep compared the two tests, "Oh, no. I was off one all the way down!" Ryan laughed and later repeated the story at the dinner table.

This is one of those flashes where you catch your breath—a teachable moment, worthy of debate. Emotions are likely to run high when your teen is obliged to look at an inappropriate decision. You can turn the situation around and lead them to better choices in the future as they gain strength from your clear expectations.

Five Techniques for Challenge

- Express your concern without beginning the sentence with "You."

- Keep the message clear and direct.

- Ask what they could say or do to prevent it from happening again.

- Look and sound confident while maintaining eye contact.

- Express surprise that they would have chosen to make this decision.

When you suspect that things aren't what they appear, trust your instincts and probe for more details. Your teen may be in an impossible situation, worrying that getting out of it will mean the end of a friendship or succumbing to the pressure.

At two in the morning, Seth's friend Glenn called several girls he knew to sneak over and party. Seth was miserable, but did not want to seem like a chicken, so he pretended to get ill. Before the girls arrived, Seth called his dad in the middle of the night to pick him up from Glenn's house. He said he was sick and needed to come home. In the car, his father quietly asked his distraught son if he would like to talk about it.

Five Tips to Probe

- Use subtlety when leading into the conversation.
- Ask open-ended questions without asking too many.
- Listen between the lines for what's not being said.
- Avoid assuming. If you do not understand, clarify.
- Practice patience and explore slowly with an unruffled voice.

When your teen exposes their frightened heart, treat it with the tenderness and the loving support a friend would show you. Samantha had been dating Mick for three weeks when she began to hear gossip about how "far" she'd gone on her dates. Horrified, Samantha searched to discover who was responsible for the scuttlebutt. As it turned out, one of her best friends, Mandy, was spreading the rumor.

Seven Tricks to Show Support

- Demonstrate an interest in helping without taking over.
- Separate your feelings from your teen's to remain calm and able to help.
- Share a story of a similar situation in your life.
- Talk about normal joys and struggles.
- Ask your teen if they would like your advice.
- Express good feelings that your teen will make a worthy choice.
- Keep your teen's confidences.

The Art of Verbal Fencing

Your teen has found their voice. They argue like a diplomat for greater privileges, choices, and independence. As your teen matures, a greater vocabulary develops, which they test through challenging debates with you. You may not plan to argue with your teen, but find yourself sucked into verbal contests that seem to go round and round. This confusing dialogue is frustrating and often ends with nothing satisfactorily accomplished.

What is your teen really asking and how should you respond? Are they testing their ability to reason, or is there an underlying message holding the true meaning? Your teen may feel pressure from friends to do things they're not ready for or don't even like. Your teen may be looking to you to stop them and help them save face with their friends by saying "My parents won't let me."

To find out what your teen is really asking for, quietly listen. Rather than challenge, reflect back using some of their own words. This would sound something like: "Mom, there is no reason I shouldn't go the party. Everyone else is going!" Your response would be, "So, everyone else is going to the party, and you don't see a reason you can't go." Through active listening, you will be able to discern if there's a hidden agenda. If you chose instead to go toe-to-toe, you'd just look like the bad guy. You may sense your teen's relief that you won't let them go. Perhaps your teen was worried about finding themselves caught in an unsafe situation, but didn't know how to get out of it.

Just as a canny lawyer might, your teen has found loopholes in many of your arguments. Usually much later, you find the real reason for the debate is that they believe they're old enough to have more privileges or choices. With their escalating voice and assertive body language, you find yourself reacting by shutting down, not listening, and wanting to end the argument as quickly as possible. But debating is actually a positive sign that your teen is learning the art of negotiation. As they continue to explain their side, they can close off all avenues of saying no. If left unchecked, you might feel heckled after a relatively few short weeks. That's why you should try these techniques to create a win-win situation:

- Stay still, stay calm, and look your teen directly in the eyes.

- Listen for what is not being said, and watch your teen's body language.

- Reflect back what your teen is saying, summarizing without judgment or opinion.

- Ask your teen to be more specific: "Explain to me how this is a problem for you."

- Once satisfied they have explained their side, identify a feeling, "You're incredibly frustrated that you have to stay home when everyone else is going to the party."

- Your teen may not agree with the feeling and offer a different one instead. Reflect this feeling back to your teen.

- Explain your reasons for your decision, followed by suggesting, "Let's think together if there are some other solutions to this problem."

Talks in the Dark

Jessica came home from her date glowing with excitement. She walked into the quiet house and saw her father sitting on the couch reading, waiting for her to arrive home. "Dad! You'll never guess what happened!" After a joyful recounting of her night out, Jessica bent down to give her sleepy father a kiss. "Night, Dad," she whispered.

Compare this to the all-too-common teen scene. Jessica let herself into the dark home. Quietly, she tiptoed in to say goodnight to her sleeping parents. The next morning, Jessica stumbled into the kitchen for breakfast. While sipping coffee, her mom asked about the date. Not quite awake, Jessica grumbled, "Good." Her mom tried to ask a few more questions, but the irritation in Jessica's voice shut the conversation down.

So many times, we miss the opportunity to connect. We see teens as unreachable and inaccessible rather than looking for new ways we can become closer. Often when we want to talk to them, they don't want to talk to us. And, like most busy households, when they are ready to talk, we're often involved with something else. When raising teens, we need to find new ways to stay close.

Talks in the dark can be one of your favorite experiences with your teen. Alone, tired, and at their most vulnerable, your teen will let down their guard and allow you into their world, even if it's just for a moment. This is a time to hear your teen's hopes and dreams, worries and concerns. A moment when, for both of you, your day has finally ended and you're ready to wind down.

You can begin by softly asking gentle, oblique questions to get them talking. Try, "You seem extra tired today," or "I'm really proud of how you handled the problem at school. How did you think of that?" Learn something new about your teen without giving your opinion or suggesting ways they could have managed the situation better. This is a natural opportunity to discover their hopes and dreams, talents and interests, likes and dislikes, and friends and heroes.

The things that go bump in the night should be the sound of you connecting in a deep and meaningful way with your teen. While you're sharing this time, know they are struggling to put feelings into words and may be reluctant to express emotions. Say as little as possible. Try not to lecture or give advice. It is your teen's time to talk. Nod your head or pat them softly in response. Show you are listening by asking, "What did you do next?" If your teen shares funny stories, see the humor and laugh.

Time alone together after the house shuts down gives your teen a chance to have your undivided attention and to feel loved and worthwhile. These talks in the dark are reminiscent of your teen's early childhood, when you would cozy up at night and read bedtime stories. With everyone so busy, taking these peaceful minutes to share and listen will bring you and your teen closer than ever before. These years pass quickly and soon your teen will leave home. You will be thankful you stopped to linger, soothe, or listen. To deeply connect to your teen, talk in the dark. Here are some openers to get you started:

- "I was thinking about the time . . ."

- "I've done that before."

- "That happened to me, too."

- "Do you remember . . ."

Resolve Conflict with Your Teen

Some conflict during adolescence is normal. Your teen may be trying on different behaviors to see what works and what doesn't or is arguing as a way to discharge tension. The arguments may be over simple things like clothes or a messy room. At times, it probably seems your teen is challenging every household rule.

As a parent, you may be concerned about the number of arguments you are having with your teen. If conflict occurs more than three times per week, the intensity is raised to yelling, and the good feelings you have for one another are interrupted for longer than two days, it has become a problem.

Choose to stop patterns that are ineffective. Shift from who is right and who is wrong to compromise. State the problem as you see it, and listen without interrupting when your teen describes it. Let them know how the conflict affects you. "When you're shouting, I have difficulty understanding what you're trying to say."

Mentally set a time limit of thirty minutes to discuss a problem. After this amount of time, if nothing has been accomplished, agree to take a break, setting a time to reopen the discussion later in the day. It takes twenty minutes to cool off after an argument and to regain composure. However, this cooldown period only happens if you distract yourself from thinking about the conflict, allowing your emotions to return to normal.

Teach your teen to fight fairly through role modeling and agreed-upon limits. Ban all zingers, name-calling, or blaming, and request that they show respect even if they don't feel like it. One of your greatest gifts can be to teach your teen to take responsibility for their own feelings. "I will not fight with you. I am going to my room. When you are ready to talk without yelling, come get me."

Uncover all the ways you can reduce daily battles. Decide what is really important and what is not. Creatively find new ways to approach problems. "I found your clean clothes on the floor with all your dirty ones. Can you help me figure out how we can fix this?" Or, "Your bedtime is eleven o'clock, but I often find you on the Internet after that time. Without changing your bedtime, do you have any ideas how we can solve this?"

To eliminate daily skirmishes over the small stuff, write a contract that clearly outlines expectations and consequences. Here's how:

- State positively and specifically all expected chores and behavior.

- Have your teen create the list of consequences for each request not honored.

- Give redeemable tickets or points for each chore or behavior accomplished.

- Make sure that consequences are immediate, appropriate, and executed as pleasantly as possible.

To reduce conflict between you and your teen, try these general tips:

- Speak calmly, but firmly.

- Keep your cool.

- Take many pauses to allow your teen to speak.

- If you have difficulty resolving a problem, write a letter to make your point.

- Allow your teen to be angry without trying to fix it, but have them do it in their room.

- Make a conscious effort to talk things over on a regular basis.

Defuse an Angry Mood

Although anger temporarily disrupts your relationship, helping your teen work through their emotions will keep you connected even in the rough times. When your teen feels out of control, they will look to you to be their anchor amidst the turbulence. By stepping back, remaining calm, and not reacting, you will be able to view every angry mood as another opportunity for your teen to practice coping with their frustrations.

Your teen's self-talk, or what they tell themselves about a situation, is a key to their escalating mood. Are they telling themselves that someone has purposely harmed them or made them afraid or embarrassed them in front of others? Is your teen repeating these words with increasing intensity or even more negative self-talk? As your teen internally repeats words that create a powerful energy, their heart beats more rapidly, their breathing becomes shallow, and an anxious fluttering begins in their chest.

Fortunately, they have you as a caring parent to help them become aware of these initial signals so they can interrupt their line of thinking before a moody outburst. When you notice your teen's temper is building, have them immediately stop right where they are and exhale using their stomach muscles. By exhaling without inhaling, your teen will slow down their heart rate as well as the rush of adrenaline that anger stirs up. After exhaling, ask your teen what they're saying to themselves at that very moment.

The most difficult part of teaching your teen to monitor their self-talk is convincing them that what they think creates their mood. Pick a time when your teen is calm and relaxed. Ask them how they can tell when they're angry. You can prompt them by asking, "Do you feel it anywhere in your body?" Or, "I notice when I'm upset, my heart beats faster. Does yours?" If your teen still has difficulty recalling physical symptoms when experiencing anger, have them bring to mind an event they found particularly distressing and identify where they feel the emotion. Is it in their head, heart, chest, or stomach? Becoming aware of bodily reactions to escalating anger is the first step toward them learning to interrupt their mood.

You can also teach your teen a feeling vocabulary, so they have the language to identify and express confusing emotions beyond the words "happy," "sad," "mad," and "afraid." This is particularly helpful if you have an especially sensitive teen. Learning new words like "embarrassed," "frustrated," "disappointed," and "anxious" develops a feeling language, which is essential to your teen's relationships now and in the future.

It takes about four to six weeks to make significant changes in dealing with anger. Your teen can begin by using self-soothing phrases like, "I will remain calm," "I can choose how I act," and "I'm responsible for my anger."

Anger is learned, but so is calming down. Have your teen make a list of what calms them down and post it in their room. Many teens suggest that the following techniques work for them:

- Put on a headset and listen to music.

- Write poetry or keep a feeling journal.

- Engage in a physical activity by going for a walk or dancing to loud music.

- Tear a piece of paper into little pieces.

- Take a hot bath or shower.

- Use a punching bag in the garage.

- Call a friend.

Finding Fresh Approaches

Heather enjoyed running car pool for her son's swim-team practices. It was one of the few moments in her teen's life that she could be present but invisible. As Heather drove her son and his friends to the pool, they would forget she was listening. Engaging in a teasing banter, they would talk about the latest incident at school, who was dating whom, and the problems they had in their classes. Many times Heather had to bite her tongue to keep from commenting or offering advice. She had learned early on that this was the surest way to shut down any revealing conversation. Heather had learned the fine art of lying low to learn more about her son's life and social scene.

Make your home a haven for teens by providing snacks and private space with a variety of entertainment. Bring them into the kitchen with warm brownies and feed their friends. Nothing gets dialogue going more than lots of teen food in the kitchen. You may even hear more than you want to know. A little prompting with cookies goes a long way to encourage teen talk and laughter.

As parents we have a tendency to continue to use the same old methods when interacting with our teens. Perhaps these techniques work with other family members or were successful when you were being raised. Take a fresh look at how you are conducting your role as a parent. Separate your feelings from your teen's behavior and concentrate on stepping back to look objectively at the way you set limits and the way you initiate change. Experiment, explore, and discover unusual and unique ways to raise your teen during these sometimes trying years. Try out new solutions to old problems. Invent an original way to communicate.

When you make a change, there will be a ripple effect, and your teen will need to learn new ways to behave with you. Deepen your connection through time spent together, active listening, and words of appreciation. Know in your heart that your greatest desire is to create a rich relationship that lasts your lifetime.

Here are some fresh approaches to try:

- Nix what is not working, and don't try fixing what's not broken.

- When giving direction, say it in as few words as possible.

- Listen more and talk less.

- Keep a dialogue going on a daily basis, not just in crisis.

- Spend time together exploring one of your teen's interests.

- Model respect, appreciation, and acceptance.

- Take a parent "time-out" when angry.

- Schedule one evening together as a family as well as one-on-one time.

- Talk while doing something else together. This will be a time when your teen's guard is down.

- Keep a list of jobs that they can do to earn extra privileges.

- Visualize a successful, happy, and centered teen, especially when they're not.

Open the Door to Humor

Teens have a wonderful sense of what is funny, and they're not afraid to be silly. Their days are happier when they feel connected to the world through humor. I've heard many teens say, "I feel great when I'm with my friends. We hang out, play music real loud, and laugh a lot." Endorphins rise when teens laugh, causing their moods to stabilize and strengthening them against stress. Concentration also improves and small irritations don't seem as bad when you've been laughing. The tension at home dissipates and an ease settles over the house.

What boys find funny is often vastly different from what girls do. Your son may tease you with a play on words or ask questions he knows you have no idea how to answer. He will play clever pranks and expect them to be played on him as well. Your daughter may giggle when you do something funny and tell her friends. In fact, she may even copy you! It's probably unusual for her to tell jokes, but she'll gladly play tricks on her friends. She enjoys sitting around in groups and laughs over high-school tales.

One mother borrowed a friend's chicken costume for Halloween. As a joke, she wore the headpiece when she went to pick her freshman son up at school. As she sat in the crowed parking lot with the fuzzy chicken head on, her son and his friends walked slowly up to the car. Her son didn't noticed his mother until his friend said, "What does your mother have on her head?" Half-horrified and half-laughing, her son shouted, "Mommmm, don't *ever* come to the school like this again!"

If your teen is not humorous by nature, you can teach them to be. Find humor rather than humiliation when an absurdity occurs in your life. Describe it to your teen in ways they can identify with. Release tension or defuse a mood with a quick quip. In the midst of holiday pictures, when all his siblings were complaining and picking on one another, one teen said in a loud voice, "Family picture day stinks!" Everyone laughed, the mood of the group changed, and great pictures were taken.

Laugh at yourself and tell funny or embarrassing stories. Sit around the dinner table and describe something funny that happened that day. Ask your teen to search their memory and tell a story. At first, they may struggle with the telling, but before long, they'll enjoy engaging you all with funny tales. Laughing as a family will minimize the pain of a disappointment and help your teen step outside a potentially negative situation.

By opening the door to humor, you'll help your family connect through a playful attitude and the ability to laugh deeply at the same things. Humor will help everyone feel like they belong and can rise above troubles together.

Here are some tips to help tickle your family's funny bone:

- Cut out comics from the paper to tape to the refrigerator.

- Tell an embarrassing story about yourself with laughter in your voice.

- Watch a funny movie together.

- Focus on a part of any story they can identify with as funny in their own life.

- Have a play on words, laugh at mistakes, and smile when your teen is grumpy.

- Regard humorous teachings as a part of psychological health and well-being.

The Response You Receive Is the Message You Send

As our children grow older, the way we communicate with them often dramatically changes, moving from compassion to commands. When they were two years old and came in the house crying with a scraped knee, we would say with great sympathy, "Oh, did you fall down?" Then, as a preschooler, "Oh no, that must have hurt. Let me get a Band-Aid." In grade school, "Wow, that hurt. Let's clean it up and tie your shoes so that it doesn't happen again." In middle school, "Put a Band-Aid on. If you keep your shoes tied, you won't trip." As a teen, the empathy sometimes turns into a demand, "Tie your shoes."

What seems like efficient communication is now regularly perceived by your teen as ordering, blaming, and disapproval. The lines of connection are crossed. This difficulty in speaking the same language comes at a time when your teen is preoccupied with their stress and their life. What they perceive you said and what you actually have said may be vastly different. When you have to mention something minor and say, "Mark, I need to talk to you," does he reply, "Am I in trouble?"

Discover where your messages may lose their intended meaning. Take a step back and check if you are giving more orders than making requests. Is there a familiar annoyance in your voice? Are you doing more lecturing than reciprocal expressing? Are you treating your teen with the same respect you would a friend, or are you cutting your teen off when they challenge you?

There is a ripple effect in communication. Two people can't interact in the same old way if one does something different, no matter how minuscule. Finding a middle ground, one where you're both satisfied and happy with your way of relating, will avoid point/counterpoint quarrels and minimize some of the "attitude" of your teen. You might confide in your teen and say, "This is the first time I have raised a teen. It's all new to me, too." Make sure all your communication is direct, without a hidden agenda or underlying meanings. If you have something important you need to discuss with your teen, plan it out first, so your questions can convey trust and consideration. Speak quietly but firmly, and be sure your tone matches your words and body language.

Ensure when you give a compliment that you don't unwittingly take it away, "Thanks for cleaning your bathroom, but you forgot to wash around the faucets." Save this caveat for tomorrow. Slow down your speech, watch for pressure on your words, and make more statements like, "Let's see if we can make this work."

You are tutoring your teen on how to talk so others will listen. Keep your messages short and simple, infused with loving-kindness. Our greatest leaders are our strongest empathizers.

Try these suggestions to help you give the right message:

- Talk to your teen as a real person, a friend.

- Give direct answers to direct questions.

- Become your teen's sounding board.

- Keep your tone of voice pleasant and relaxed.

- Remove all "you's" when discussing something that needs to be changed.

- Teach them to do something different without arguing, like composing their thoughts in an e-mail and sending it to you.

Take Advantage of an Unexpected Connection

Think back to when you were a teen. What are your most memorable moments? Who was there and what were you doing? Call to mind these special pictures and remember the images, scents, and feelings. More than likely, your parents and siblings are a part of many beloved memories.

Debra recalls standing in front of the large picture window with her mother just before Christmas and her fifteenth birthday. It was close to midnight, and all the lights had been turned off. The snow was falling in large flakes in a whisper of wind. "Remember this day," said her mother. "We are standing in our home, you in your pink nightgown, and me in my blue. We're watching each snowflake drift down from the sky, each one as unique as you. Whenever you see new snow falling, remember this day." Debra's mother took advantage of an unexpected connection.

Opportunities come up each day, but we are often too busy to stop and notice. Most of the time, you are the one doing the asking and when your teen refuses, it can be quite exasperating. You've asked repeatedly if they would like to go on an errand, out for a bite to eat, or to see a movie. You may feel like you have exhausted all your ideas as you try to find new ways to connect. However, when you look closely, you suddenly realize that all of your requests have been built into *your* time frame instead of your teen's. From this day forward, decide to make yourself 100 percent available to the next opening your teen presents.

Many opportunities happen as you're passing through a room or getting ready for bed. Your teen might blurt out something unexpectedly, just at the moment you think you are too tired to have another coherent thought. Maybe your teen is hanging around the house, staying close, and turning down their friends to go out. Are they giving you a message that they want to spend time with you?

You may not realize you have an invitation until long afterward. Every Tuesday, Toni would watch *Teen Idol* on TV. One evening, Toni's mother decided to stop rushing around and join her. Tuesdays soon became a regular ritual, and conjointly they began to look forward to the excitement of a shared show and an evening together.

Start creating unexpected connections with these simple tips:

- If your teen initiates a connection, stop what you're doing, if only briefly.

- Ask, "Do you want to talk about it?"

- Read the same book.

- Watch MTV and talk about the songs.

- Take the day off from work to get their driver's license.

Listen with Your Heart

Travis's girlfriend, Jill, had broken up with him, and no matter how his friends and family tried to console him, Travis was devastated. For weeks, he walked around with a long look on his face and a breaking sadness in his voice. His parents' emotions went from concern to frustration as they saw Travis fall deeper into his sadness. One day, his mother, worn out by the constant low mood, sat wearily on the couch opposite her son, who seemed to stare blankly at the TV. She said in a whisper, "It hurts, doesn't it Travis?" Slowly nodding his head, Travis began talking—about the pain, rejection, and the fear that he would never love anyone else the way he'd loved Jill. Rather than give assurances or advice, his mother quietly listened with her heart. She heard the feeling behind each word as Travis struggled to make sense of it all.

Every teen needs to tell their story to someone who cares, to be heard without opinion, belittling, or advice. For you to listen without judgment is a blessing. It helps your teen believe they are worthwhile, necessary, and loved. When you listen with your heart, your teen realizes they don't have to go it alone, and that you're a person to be trusted.

To listen with your heart, you must be emotionally, physically, and mentally present. Be still, stop moving about the house, turn off all distractions, and give your teen your full attention. Watch your teen's body language and focus on the feelings behind the words. Concentrate on what your teen is saying, rather than thinking of what you want to say next. Avoid interpreting and accept their feelings without trying to change them or giving suggestions.

When the only sound you hear in the room is your teen's voice, you will become aware of the beating of your own heart and your rhythmic, relaxed breathing. Time will seem to have stopped and the love flowing between the two of you will increase with each passing moment. You can tell you have truly connected when your teen begins to turn their body, leaning toward you in hope and healing.

You are giving of yourself and "being there" in the purest sense. Listening in this way is like wrapping your arms around your teen's spirit and sharing the unconditional love you have for them. It may not solve the immediate problem, but when you seek to understand, it helps open unlimited possibilities to resolve their unhappiness.

To be truly heard is one of our greatest needs as human beings. We strive to be heard. We *need* to be heard. For our sons, we give them the gift of receiving compassion and a language to describe their experience. For girls, we teach them to express and let go, rather than holding on to an accounting for each transgression made against them.

By simply listening this way, you're offering love, caring, and a chance to deepen your relationship. Freeze this moment, as it will last a lifetime between you. It may mean the difference between carrying a scar and letting pain go. This time is brief and passes quickly. To connect deeply with your teen, listen with your heart.

PART 4

From Crib to Car: Why Does Your Teen Need So Much Space?

Embracing the "Prickly Pear"

Once upon a time, there was a darling, tender, cuddly child who welcomed and returned all the love the queenly mother and kingly father could bestow upon them. As the years passed, this bundle of pleasure matured and ripened into a new hybrid species, the "Prickly Pear." The child became a teenager with a thick, thorny outer covering that discouraged most nurturing embraces or caresses. The royal couple was distraught, confused, and sometimes annoyed with this new exotic fruit that appeared to reject all their efforts.

Parent/child relationships undergo an enormous transformation when entering teen years. The "prickly pear" outer covering is the boundary your teen has erected between you and them. Although they want you close, your teen may feel your hugs and warmth are no longer necessary and has not yet matured enough emotionally to gracefully accept your affection. They may regard these good-faith attempts as intrusive or even as gross. At times, they'll crave a hug or embrace, but these moments seem pretty random. For the general well-being and health of your teenager, establishing and maintaining physical closeness is a noble and worthy quest.

To do the dance, take lessons to learn the steps to connect during adolescence. It is your teen's job to challenge your attempts to show affection, and they take this job seriously! The trick is to recognize when your efforts or tactics are off course or unwelcome. If you have previously established a physically expressive relationship with your teen, you may have an easier go at maintaining some avenue of positive exchange. On the other hand, both you and your teen may experience more intense emotions and conflict as the separation process continues, which now must accommodate a physical distance.

Your teen may not feel comfortable with obvious signs of affection, but may reciprocate in other ways. Your son may show his affection toward you by picking you up in front of his friends or squeezing you too tight. And your daughter may express her love by letting you hug her without hugging you. Your teen might say, "Love you, Mom," as they slip out the door before you can give an "I love you" back.

Evaluate and test your teen's tolerance and acceptance of your embrace. They may only consent to a pat on the shoulder, a brief hug, or a stroke of their hair. You must negotiate both verbally and by observation what your teen will accept. "If you feel uncomfortable with me getting in your space with a hug or kiss, in what way would it be okay to show my affection?" Ask how they'd like you to express your delight and interest in their life, including when, where, and in front of whom. Having ongoing conversations with your teen may lessen the misunderstandings and increase the satisfaction of all.

Affection, admiration, comfort, and love will always be a vital part of your teen's well-being, even if they don't think so. The first step is to ask permission, "Can I give you a hug?" If denied, try again at a different time in another situation. This is a passing phase, and soon your teen will once again look to you for comfort and love. This tender relationship you are fostering will require insight, perseverance, and patience. Start now to establish an ongoing effort of steady affection and hugs. Try these simple suggestions:

- Always go to your teen's bedroom for a good-night kiss (don't forget to knock).

- Reach out in affection when your teen is happy, excited, or joyful.

- When your teen is distraught ask, "Would you like a hug?"

- Say "I love you" every time your teen leaves the house.

Discover Where You End and Your Teen Begins

Since your teen was born, you've sustained an attachment or bond that is like a solid steel drum. For many years, it seemed like nothing could even scratch the surface of this connection, but now your child has grown older and is struggling to create a new, defined self. During adolescence, it's natural for your teen to ask, "Who am I?" and "How am I different from my parents?" This is the most important task in adolescent development and the foundation for forming your teen's own identity.

Your teen needs your approval to separate, just as they once needed your permission to cross the street. They need absolute acceptance from you to have a separate, individual identity, one where they are able to think independently, learn from mistakes, and risk making new ones. By adopting a willingness to change with your teen, you can grow together. Say aloud, "I like the way you handled that. Could you show me how?"

Despite you allowing them to develop independence and create a new identity, they still need your help toward this new self. Be there when their world is falling apart or when they have made a foolish error. Through these experiences, they will gain self-respect and won't need to pretend to be someone they're not. During this growing period, they are learning about themselves and trying on new roles. Many will be discarded while a few will merit further investigation.

The more secure and confident your teen feels, the more they can individualize from the family. Stay forever connected by helping them draw the line between where you end and they begin.

Check out these signs that your teen has healthy boundaries:

- They develop close friendships.

- They can and do distinguish between their own feelings and those of others.

- They move toward goals and desires.

- They know how to get needs met in a healthy way.

Learning how to set and maintain healthy boundaries and develop as an individual is a process, and your teen may not totally have it down yet. To help them get the hang of it, try implementing these strategies:

- Have your teen take responsibility for their thinking, feeling, and behavior.

- Build up their "street smarts" to ensure awareness when in unsafe situations.

- Set a baseline for their physical space by walking slowly toward them until they are uncomfortable. Have them identify this uncomfortable feeling.

- Practice out loud what to say and do if someone is making them uncomfortable by pushing past a boundary.

See the Forest As Well As the Teen

Tori arrived at the high school to pick up her son. After waiting twenty minutes, she walked into the courtyard to look for him. Approaching a large circle of students, she asked the boys if they had seen her son, Jake. Right next to her, Tori heard a deep voice say, "I'm right here, Mom." Her son, with his spiked hair, baggy pants, and T-shirt, had totally blended in with the entire group! She had walked right up and never recognized him.

What we "see" and "hear" is a state of mind. Our perceptions rule our thoughts. When the word "teenager" is said, other parents sagely nod their heads in sympathy. A vivid image has arisen of adolescent turmoil, confusion, and mood swings. As much as your teen strives to be like their friends, they want you to regard them as unique and having a special purpose in the world. Take advantage of a refreshing way to connect with your teen by envisioning them as an individual rather than simply as part of a group, discovering their hopes, dreams, and passions.

You may find yourself worrying whether your teen will turn out well. More than likely, the answer is a resounding "yes." What is the big picture? Are they primarily a good kid? If so, slow down your anxiety and look beyond the forest to who your teen really is becoming. Consider their strengths instead of their weaknesses. Maintain an individualized approach.

Even though your teen's music is loud and it vibrates the floor, it's not who they are, but what they like to listen to. Some of the posters in their room may be shocking to you, but underneath these alarming forms of art lies the kind heart of your teen. Remember that they help others who need it and listen when they are tired. They are known for being there for friends and often being thoughtful and considerate. Your teen chooses more wisely than you fear, but doesn't always let you know it.

Your relationship has been good and there is no reason for it to be different now. When your fears get in the way of your positive view, envision your teen in the future—successful, happy, and gracious. Here are some ways to start:

- Take a moment to hold a beautiful vision of your teen.

- Regard them as unique and special.

- Recognize their good qualities that are different from those of their friends.

- Help them discover a sense of purpose.

- Fan the fire in their belly to go out and conquer the world.

Teach Refusal Skills

As a parent, your biggest fear may be how to teach your teen to say no in the face of strong pressure. You hope that through your years of influence, your teen understands how to stay away from damaging activities or walk away when challenged.

Teaching your teen refusal skills takes a commitment to persevere despite the negative barrage by the media and your best friends' well-meaning advice. Remember, as a parent you can still be a powerful enough influence to sway even the shakiest teen. Begin not with warnings of danger, but by talking about how they don't need to go along to have friends. Tell a story from your own past or someone else's describing the struggle between taking a stand and going along.

Your adolescent feels a tremendous need to be part of a crowd, to have a sense of belonging. Friends influence whether your teen feels likeable, important, and attractive. As much as you'd like to believe your teen should get this self-confidence from the family, they will still desire the crowd's affirmation. So how do you teach your teen to not go along with the crowd and dare to be different? How do you explain that they have the right to say no and set boundaries that will last a lifetime?

Your teen will become who you prophesize them to be. You can predict future behavior by strengthening your teen's positive view of themselves. Teaching refusal skills is more than telling your teen to say no. You need to show them through words, affection, and body language that they have a purpose greater than an immediate thrill. By becoming your teen's mirror, you can reflect back your belief in their resourcefulness and ability to make quality decisions.

It can be both frightening and exhilarating to be confronted with temptations. If your teen is not prepared or practiced in ways to handle the pressure, they may blindly leap into a bad situation by believing there is no other alternative. Teach your teen to think, "What kinds of things don't I want to do?" "What are the consequences?" "Is the person pressuring me?" If the answer is yes, ask your teen to picture a red flag waving a warning sign of danger.

Coach your teen to avoid angry tones or put-downs while saying no, since other teens will react with more intensity and defend what they want to do. Instead, they can give a strong nonverbal message such as a shake of the head or standing stiff with arms crossed. Encourage your teen to store an excuse in their memory, like "I'm not into that." Explore ways to avoid the situation or support your teen in finding a new, more accepting crowd. Most importantly, help your teen set personal goals. If your teen has a clear picture of their future, you can predict a life of confidence, certainty, and hope.

Steps to Saying No

1. Say the person's name and make direct eye contact while you identify the trouble. ("Austin, you want to skip school.")

2. Clarify with a question. ("You want me to cut class and leave?")

3. State the personal consequences. ("If I do that, I'll be kicked off the team.")

4. Suggest an alternative. ("Instead, let's just go to the mall after school.")

5. If the person continues to pressure, leave.

Give Calm to Chaos

From the sound of the alarm until the time your teen's head hits the pillow at night, their days are spent moving quickly from one distraction to another. There is little time for childhood routines that once gave stability amidst the confusion. If you are watching in suspense for your teen to grow into a calm adult, you may have a long wait. However, you can create new habits that bring order back to your household.

You can reestablish comforting practices by regarding your family as a whole system whose interactions and behavior influence the serenity in your home. Spend one week writing down every family member's activity in as much detail as possible. Then examine this list for things you can eliminate, activities you can bring routine to, and changes that could be made to enhance harmony within your home.

Include eating dinner at relatively the same time every day, with everyone as a group cleaning up, putting away food, and washing dishes. Keep the same routine for each person to establish a pattern that is automatic rather than autocratic. If your teen snacks after dinner, have them put their dishes in the dishwasher and wash the counter so you don't wake up to another mess. Set out a xeroxed list of chores with check marks by the ones you expect your teen to complete that day.

Shut down the TV early in the evening to reduce the volume of noise in your home. Encourage more time in quiet activities like reading and visiting. Create a space for your teen to study with supplies easily within reach. Ensure a specific study time is set each day when they're not disturbed by siblings, friends, or telephone calls. If they say, "But I have no homework," have them sit in their space and read for one hour or work on a project. It will quickly remove the "no homework" blues.

Leave paper or an erasable board with attachable pens near the telephone to record all messages. Whoever listens to the answering machine is responsible for listing the information accurately. Each family member is then instructed to check the list for the details. Require your teen to also use this message board to let you know where they're going and with whom. Remember to model the same courtesy by leaving them notes about where you've gone and what time you will be back.

If your teen is driving, have them wash, wax, and vacuum the car every Saturday. Make this a time when they fill the car with gas to prevent rushing to the gas station late at night. Teach them how to get the car serviced, change a tire, and pay for any driving infractions to increase their level of responsibility.

Schedule a time each week to spend with your teen, letting them know you're setting these hours aside to enjoy their company. Unless there is a crisis, keep your commitment—this will tell them just how important they are to you. You may have to leave the house to avoid distractions, yet you can still keep these outings simple and cheap.

If your teen is having a particularly anxious day, have them practice progressive-relaxation techniques. Teach them to lie down with eyes closed, imagining a red spot of warmth starting at the tip of their toes and spreading up their body until they are completely relaxed. At this point, have them imagine a place where they've felt happy and peaceful and say to themselves, "I am relaxed, I am successful, and I feel good."

A calm home takes conscious effort and time, but once the foundation is established, harmony will continue to give your teen a safe haven in a chaotic world.

Change Your Labels

Your teen will become who you predict them to be. Tell them they're smart, good, and trustworthy, and your teen will grow up believing they are all these things. They'll live life accordingly, as if what you told them was true.

Sandra was raising a willful daughter, who, by the age of thirteen, was able to reduce her mother to tears of frustration on a nearly daily basis. One day, as Sandra bitterly complained to her own mother, her mom replied, "Rachel isn't difficult. She has an artistic personality that makes her especially sensitive to her environment." From that small exchange, Sandra began to change her perception of her daughter from challenging to highly responsive. Now twenty years old, Rachel enjoys a wonderfully close and loving relationship with her mother.

Treat your teen as the person you want them to become. Even after they behave badly, you can say, "Allison, this surprises me. You're usually so thoughtful and kind." Turn labels like "crabby" into "expressive," or "critical" into "accurate." By reframing this way, you'll find that the way you view your teenager will undergo a remarkable transformation.

If you want your teen's behavior to change, act as if it already has. Show this in your choice of words, body language, and tone. When you're concerned that they may make a poor choice, say, "I know you'll do the right thing. You always do." As you raise the bar, your teen's expectations of themselves will change, too.

Give your teen a clean slate to start fresh. Begin by looking for the good in your teen every day. Notice when they are kind, thoughtful, and responsible. Say affirming statements to yourself as often as possible and in the present, as if they were already true. Before too long, these words will be imprinted on your mind and positively affect your interactions with your teen. Here are some examples you can start with:

- "I have a wonderful teen."

- "We are getting closer every day."

- "When they debate, they are testing their ability to negotiate."

- "I am so glad they're alive."

- "The teen years are my favorite stage."

- "Each day, I'm noticing what is great about my teen."

- "I love my teen with all my heart."

Now try these techniques to help you change your labels about your teen:

- Make an exhaustive list of all the great qualities your teen possesses, then look for one of these characteristics each day.

- Positively encourage more of these behaviors.

- Label a problem as a challenge.

- Put a positive spin on a negative event.

- Don't take behavior personally.

How to Hang Out

Some of your best moments with your teen will be when you connect while hanging out. As your teen moves from adolescence into adulthood, they'll need less formal parenting and more of a relationship with you. To encourage this friendship and closeness as the years unfold, discover fun ways to relate to your teen.

Having a teen in the house means you're probably spending more time managing and monitoring than you are having fun. When your child was little, you would get down on the floor and play whatever silly game or activity they were enjoying. Now, with work pressures, minimal free time, and often limited resources, "playing" with your teen might seem more of a chore than a pleasure. This is especially true if your teen is involved with multiple activities.

It takes creative energy to capture the interest of your busy teen, but being playful allows your teen to see you differently—as a person they can relate to. Uncover the time you both have free and have a list of activities you can do at a moment's notice. You may want to schedule your teen into your calendar just as you would with a client or an appointment. Be sure to ask your teen if this works for them, and then stick to this time frame. If something unexpected occurs, make every effort to keep your time together sacred. By saying no to other requests and honoring your commitment, your teen will also realize just how special they are to you. If the situation is not within your control, be sure to reschedule rather than drop the fun.

Even if it's just going out to lunch after an appointment or a quick trip to the mall, your teen will appreciate the undivided attention. Try to make these events one-on-one. A third person in the mix dramatically changes the dynamics of the interaction and often prevents your teen from doing or saying what they're really feeling. Get physical. One family on Thanksgiving plays football before their big meal. They don't have many players, but the running and laughter make the day more memorable. During such special times together, set aside problems and make play the priority.

Here are some fun ways to connect with your teen. Try doing these together to connect:

- Walk down the hall with a notebook ring in your nose.

- Go to the airport and pretend to greet people.

- Speak in a fake foreign tongue.

- Challenge your teen to a game of billiards.

- Play a video game.

- Lay out on a blanket in August and watch shooting stars.

- Be your teen's audience as they try on new clothes.

- Go to a concert and stop for a snack afterwards.

- Rake a big pile of fall leaves and jump into the middle.

- Shoot some baskets, even if you don't know how (a great cause for laughter).

- Take a hike or backpack up the nearest mountain or trail.

- Train for a sporting event together.

- Create a scavenger hunt for your teen and their friends.

- Go to a music store and let your teen educate you on their favorite types of music.

- Have a water-balloon fight on a hot summer day.

Keep Showing Up

A call came from Pete's math teacher. She wanted to be sure his parents knew their son was receiving an award at a ceremony on Friday. His parents were shocked. Not only hadn't they known there was a ceremony on Friday, but they'd had no idea Pete was receiving an award! Without saying a word, Pete's parents took the time off from work and showed up in one of the front rows. As Pete walked across the stage, his parents stood up and applauded. Surprised, Pete blushed, smiling as he walked off the stage.

As much as your teen emphatically states that you don't need to come, show up and clap loudly. They may complain that you're embarrassing them in front of their friends, but secretly your teen is delighted. They may also tell you that none of the other parents are going to come to take pictures, but insist that you'll be there anyway. Tell your teen that although they may not need you to be there, it's important to you.

Be a constant, supportive presence in their life. Go to their games, plays, or events. Sign up for lock-in after graduation or serve refreshments at a school event. Get involved in your teen's high school, either in the PTA or on a committee. See if there are ways you can assist the teachers or the school librarian, and become acquainted with principals, school counselors, and coaches. Organize bake sales, sew banners for the team, or create signs for buses. Share the responsibility of team manager with several other parents. If you don't have time, volunteer to make calls or send e-mails. Have spaghetti dinners at your house the night before an event to get to know the other parents and teens.

Invite grandparents, aunts, uncles, and cousins to demonstrate a network of belonging through family support. Try to look interested and smile a lot, even if you feel bored or tired. Act as if this is the most important occasion you have ever attended. One mother, to her son's horror, used to yell, "Go, Honey!" at his hockey games. Yet, at the state tournament, his teammates asked his mother to stand in the defensive zone, since many of their parents couldn't make it and they liked the encouragement.

There is a positive connection between your level of involvement in your teen's life and their personal and academic achievement. For your teen to remember all the times you loved them without being asked, keep showing up.

Here are some great ways to show support:

- Invite parents over for picture taking before a dance.

- Go to a school play, even if your teen isn't in it.

- Be their personal cheerleader, and cheer for everyone else as well.

- Attend some events and games of your teen's friends.

- Hang around after an event, especially if they lose.

- Take pictures at all their events.

- Bring your teen flowers or a gift to celebrate an honors event.

- Give high fives, pats on the back, or big hugs after each event, both public and private.

Discover a Shared Passion

Matt's life revolved around school, his friends, and his profound love of hockey. In the winter, he spent every afternoon going to the local arena to play a pick-up game. Never wanting to miss his favorite professional games on TV, he recorded each one and watched them after the house was asleep. He wore woolen hockey beanies (hats), had jerseys of his favorite players, and taped posters on his bedroom wall. Each morning while eating breakfast, Matt would read the most recent statistics in the paper and talk about them endlessly.

Lots of parents might regard the amount of energy and time Matt put into hockey as a waste. They might even want him to drop this "preoccupation" and focus on his grades or do volunteer work. In truth, many parents miss the incredible opportunity to develop a deep and lifelong connection with their teen through the unfolding of a shared passion.

If you look closely at your teen's interests, you'll find at least one pastime where you can come together. You might need to be the student and your teen the teacher. This can be a great relationship builder, letting them educate and lead you to a greater understanding. Then you can find other ways to build upon your knowledge. For instance, if you were Matt's parent, you could connect in the following ways. Try watching hockey on television or, as a special treat, go to a professional game together. Have your teen point out the intricacies of the sport and let their enthusiasm inspire you. You can read books or discover information on the Internet so you can confidently discuss all aspects with your teen. Learn to unfold an excitement for the sport, simply because you love your child. The effort you spend will tell your teen just how important they are to you.

An added benefit is that the best discussions often occur while you're involved in an activity together. Your teen won't feel pushed and there will be a noticeable ease in the flow of conversation. You will find that you are able to talk about other parts of their life, from classes to girlfriends or boyfriends.

You may choose to look for something in which you both share a curiosity. One mother, Beth, enjoyed creating greeting cards with rubber stamps. It wasn't long before she invited her artistic daughter, Jenny, to join her. For a year, they spent many happy hours at the kitchen table designing beautiful cards, which are now sold at art fairs. Recently, Jenny was contracted to produce her cards for a local gift shop.

If you're struggling to find a shared pastime, draw a line down the middle of a piece of paper. On one side, list all your hobbies and favorite pursuits. On the other side, list your teen's. Highlight the ones that are similar or that match. If you can find no common projects at this time, look carefully at your teen's list, and see if you can find something that piques your curiosity. Begin by approaching your teen with questions. Let them see true excitement and invested interest by paying close attention to their descriptions and knowledge. Show that you value the time they took to explain it to you, and uncover moments when you can spend time together on this project. Bless both of you by keeping your commitment to share their enthusiasm in a passion.

PART 5

How Much Independence Is Too Much?

Make Memories with Meals

Did you ever walk into a room and have a familiar smell trigger a warm remembrance of childhood contentment? Do you recall not being quite tall enough to look over the counter to see your mother baking cookies or standing on a chair washing dishes with a large apron across your belly? As you grew, there were special foods at holidays and celebrations with your family gathered around the dining table. Laughter and stories rang out, and there was a sense of closeness between all present. The dining room was where everyone gathered to eat, catch up, and enjoy each other's company. You can make your kitchen one of your teen's fondest memories, reminiscent of similar comfort and love.

In your fast-paced world, it may be hard to imagine how you can cook dinner, never mind teaching someone else. Meals are often rushed with everyone's activities staggered throughout the evening. Fast food is common and a balanced diet is often more luck than planned. Dishes get left in the sink, and pans have yet to be washed, discouraging even the most dedicated cook.

Invite your teen into the kitchen. Cooking side-by-side with your teen makes cooking seem less of a chore and more of a pleasure. Your teen can make a salad, create a new dish, or experiment with different spices. One teen compared a few recipes until he decided the best way to cook salmon on the grill. Enjoying his success, this teen has gone on to do a large portion of the grilling at home, which is especially enjoyable for his parents in the cold weather.

It definitely takes more time initially to teach your teen to cook, but the investment brings the dividends of a stronger relationship. Have your teen begin with something that interests them. The more pleasure your teen experiences, the greater the chance of keeping them in the kitchen.

Your teen will learn organizational skills as you teach them how to read a recipe. Show them how to measure a liquid and why they need to be accurate in baking and less so when cooking. Start with simple recipes that have fewer than six ingredients, such as roasted chicken or brownies. Show your teen how to make a grocery list recording all the products needed to make the dish. Describe a balanced meal with protein, carbohydrates, vegetables, and fruit so your teen will choose recipes more wisely. Buy them a cookbook with fast recipes that is easy to read. Once they master the basics, graduate them to more complex cookbooks as their confidence, interest, and skills expand. And, if you're not an avid cook, you can be "chefs-in-training" together.

Take this feeling of connectedness to the dinner table and make dinner conversation happen. Have a true dinner hour rather than a race to the next project. Ask about your teen's day and offer undivided attention. Here are some other suggestions to make dinner conversation lively:

- Tell funny stories.

- Ask about their favorite music.

- Appreciate their goals and dreams.

- Talk about books they've read.

- Discuss politics and current events.

- Share stories about school or work.

Holding On While Letting Go

Colin had passed his driver's test that morning and was driving alone to school for the first time. His mother walked out to the car and gave Colin a warm hug. Rather than letting go, she held on a little too tightly, knowing that with this new freedom, her son was entering a different chapter in his life. As she said goodbye, her fingers closed tightly around his arm. "Mom, you need to let go now. Mom—you need to let go. Mom! You're holding onto my arm. Please let go." With a slight chuckle and a wry grin, Colin's mother unwrapped her fingers and watched him drive off until she could no longer see his car.

There is a fine line between holding on and letting go. On one hand, you still want to be present and active in your teen's life. On the other, you want your teen to be able to leave home and make good decisions, ensuring success after high school. You wonder, "How much is enough? Can I trust my teen will make good decisions?"

It's natural to feel protective about your teen, especially since this has been your role for many years. Because of your experience, both as a teen and as a parent, you can foresee the possible perils and dangers, making it even more difficult to step back and let them go. Not all of your teen's decisions will be good ones, but by allowing them to make mistakes, they will learn important life lessons in relative safety.

Imagine a rope tied around your waist. As your teen makes more and more responsible decisions, you let out a little extra rope until finally you feel confident you can cut the cord, trusting they'll return safely. By encouraging your teen to take these steps alone, you will encourage their courageous spirit to emerge.

While your teen is growing and changing, you are also having your own developmental crisis, determining what you will do with your future. With more free time calling you from the horizon, you might want to think about how your life will be different. Think back to discover if there is something you've been waiting to do until the children were grown. Perhaps you want to explore taking a few classes, learning a new hobby, or changing careers. You might even want to take a trip with your spouse to reconnect and celebrate this new stage in your marriage.

When you feel anxious about your teen's future beginnings, start making a list of what they'll need to take to college or for their first apartment. Do some research and talk to other parents of teens. Then, slowly start to purchase these items, just like you did when preparing for your teen's birth. Think about the care packages you might send, filled with favorite treats or pictures of the family. You can write a short note for each day of the first month when they'll be gone to ward off the usual freshman homesickness.

Congratulations! You have raised a teen, kept your sanity, and hugged them as they went off to explore new freedoms. Your teen is moving from dependence to interdependence. You can only hold on with love, not handcuffs—but cookies help.

Have the Courage to Encourage Independence

Joe's dad gave him a big hug after the final box was dumped in the dorm room. "I'm so proud of you, Son," said his father, choking back tears. "You're a great kid. I know you will do well here." His father turned to go down the hall. "Hey Dad," Joe whispered. "I'll miss you, too." As hard as that moment was, Joe's father knew he had done the best job he could to prepare his son to handle the independence of a life outside his family.

Raising a self-sufficient teen requires great bravery and determination. It calls for you to gradually give up control and guide your teen through adolescence rather than manage their adolescence. These years can be a scary period when you might wonder, "Am I able to trust them to do the right thing?"

By giving increasing independence now, you'll worry less as your teen moves away from your watchful eye. Encourage them to get a job and learn to manage money. Bring them down to the bank and have them open their own account and learn how to balance their checkbook. Request that your teen put a significant portion of their earnings into a savings account for college, tithing, or emergencies. Show them how to prepare and track a monthly budget, so when money is tight, they know they can still get by.

To encourage independent thinking, sit down and work together to make a grocery list followed by a trip to the store to tutor on how to compare prices and products, including the reading of labels. And don't stop there. Have your teen bring the groceries in and unpack them, showing them how to wash all fruits and vegetables before they go into the refrigerator and freeze the meat immediately.

Open your sewing box and bring out a large needle to have your teen not only thread the eye, but sew on a button. Have them iron their own shirts and bring clothes to the dry cleaner. Watch as they learn to sort dark clothes from light and do their own laundry. Familiarize your teen with how to call a taxi, get an appliance or other item repaired, and make appointments with dentists and doctors. Show them what to take when they have a fever and the different medications to take when they have a cold.

Enlarge their self-confidence and resourcefulness to handle daily living and future dilemmas. Praise them when they try, and catch them when they fail. Award increasing independence as your teen maneuvers through these different tasks, and applaud their successes. Support your teen without giving the answers when facing new challenges. Make your teen responsible for reviewing all options and solving their own problems, only coming to you if they've exhausted all resources.

Have faith that your teen will retain the values you have taught them. Believe your teen is capable and strong. Trust in the process, knowing it's your teen's job to leave the family behind in order to enter a new world. Teach them how to not give up when a situation seems hopeless and be brave when they feel most alone. When you launch your teen, let them already have tasted their first sense of freedom.

Award Increasing Autonomy

Scott's father had attended a prestigious college for his undergraduate degree and envisioned his son going there, as well. As the time approached to visit campuses, Scott's father eagerly scheduled a tour at his college. But Scott balked and declined the invitation. It was hard for his father to let go of his dream, but he understood. Scott wanted to make his own mark without the shadow of his father.

Establishing individuality is important for emotional and psychological independence and a necessary process that can be stressful for both you and your teen. At times, it may seem like your teen is turning you down as well as your values. If you dress preppy, they may decide to dress grunge. Their room may be messy, their clothes mismatched, and their hair too long, but this rebellion is a good sign that your teen is developing normally. They are in the process of discovering what they believe in and what is important to them. Just when your teen seems to be throwing all your values out the window, you'll see a flicker of hope that ultimately they'll be okay.

Let your teen know that with autonomy come new responsibilities—not rights. Let them know that as they continue to take on new responsibilities, you will increase their privileges. These new tasks might be working ten hours a week or keeping a clean driving record. You might require that they start to pay for their own movies or trips to favorite fast food restaurants. Assign additional chores to increase their work ethic or have them take over household tasks that will enhance their ability to live independently.

Your goal is to teach your teen to become self-sufficient. This is a process that has been ongoing for many years, but takes on a new sense of urgency as your teen moves through adolescence. Let them know that for you to trust them, their behavior and choices must be predictable. As each month passes and they show consistent accountability, give them fewer rules. If they're on time and maintain contact when plans change, you can extend their curfew under special circumstances. Let them know when you've noticed they've been making good choices, and that you've decided to give them more authority over their daily life. Let them know the choices they make affect others as well.

Be consistent and avoid psychological control. Allow them to self-regulate, but if they blow it, revert back to the previous rule. Any stretching or breaking of rules is a clear indication that they're not ready.

Your goal is to raise an independent teen who can make good decisions that will positively impact their future. It takes a great deal of energy to separate. Give your teen a parachute. Here's how to start:

- Remember your own adolescence—both fears and hopes.

- Increase their responsibility to self and family.

- Provide ways your teen can problem solve and make safe decisions.

- Help your teen discern dangerous situations.

- Encourage them to think through decisions, including choices and possible consequences.

Nurture Resilience

Tony was an irritable baby and a temperamental preschooler. His mom confessed she had wondered if Tony would thrive in a better-equipped family as he threw another screaming fit. In grade school, Tony was victimized and taunted. He was the last to be chosen for games and the first to be laughed at. By middle school, Tony retreated and had no one he could call a friend. Still, Tony's mother never gave up. Through high school, she helped him every night with the mountain of homework he never seemed to finish and encouraged him to join a few after-school activities. By the time Tony went off to college, he was shy but confident. Today, Tony is a successful psychiatrist treating adolescents and children. In medical school, they discovered he had attention deficit disorder.

More than ever before, resilience is needed to protect your teen against the turmoil and tension of the world. Resilience is the strength to confront the challenges your teen will face, leading to hope for a remarkable future. Developed over time, resilience gives birth to a tough spirit that is not defeated by challenges and disappointments. It's never too late to give birth to resilience.

Research shows that teens need at least one caring adult to accept them unconditionally. This counteracts the message from others that there could be something wrong with them, and they become brave enough not to give up. You can be this person that lends them courage. Your warm parent/child relationship connects your teen to the motivation to succeed and to safekeeping in the face of adversity. The quality of your support tells your teen they are valuable and important to you. As a resilient teen, they'll come to believe that they are worthwhile. Your teen will be able to act independently of peers and won't get caught up in pleasing people or mirroring what others think of them. Not only will they learn to appreciate their individuality, your teen will also recognize and develop their greatest gifts.

By becoming your teen's advocate, you can teach them how to distinguish an issue from a problem and discover creative ways to deal with both. Teach them to reframe, seeing negative situations more positively and regarding mistakes as part of the learning process rather than as failures. Lead them to sharpen critical-thinking skills by talking about world problems and determining resolutions. Ask them, "What would you do?" without giving the answers.

Encourage your teen to participate in a minimum of two after-school activities or projects. If these options are limited, focus on community volunteering with a new commitment each semester. Giving of their time and resources will create a sense of belonging and the acquisition of admirable social skills that will last a lifetime. Never give up. Resilience is learned, and you are just the person to teach it.

A household that fosters resilience is

- Nonjudgmental
- Respectful
- Empathic
- Patient
- Supportive

- Challenging
- Goal oriented
- Trusting
- Creative
- Problem solving

- Hopeful
- Optimistic
- Self-aware
- Resourceful

Transform Fear into Action

For many parents, the adolescent years can be a time of fear. Your teen is less under your watchful eye and is enjoying more freedom than ever before. At times, you may feel like you are skiing down an icy hill with no poles. You believe this journey will eventually end well, but you're still breathless with thoughts of what could happen.

Fear can be an obstacle for parents and teens. Some parents become more protective and others work just as hard trying not to think of what could go wrong. The reality is that the world has always been a dangerous place, but the majority of teens thrive despite our worries. The difference between teens who succeed and teens who flounder is a high level of resourcefulness and a refined ability to problem solve.

Play "what if" games with your teen. "What would you do if you had a flat tire or your car broke down?" "Tell me the steps you would take if you were at a party where you were uncomfortable." "What if no one was home when you called? What would you do then?" Vary your questions and be more specific as your teen's ability to work through problems increases. You can ask, "If you were instant messaging on the Internet and a new, interesting person started communicating with you, what would you do? What would be your first step if this person wanted to get together?" "What if you were on a date and it was moving faster than you would like?" If your teen is not able to give good answers to these problems, then begin the process of teaching logic and reasoning.

Becoming resourceful is a way of thinking. As your teen's closest and most valuable connection to this world, you can help them develop the ability to create strategies to lift them out of tough situations. Present realistic scenarios that they can relate to and have them walk you through each step they'd take to resolve the problem. As they become stuck at one step, give them only two or three choices they could make to get to the next step.

When your teen encounters a new situation in life, ask them what they could have done differently and how that would have affected the outcome. Tell them stories of difficult episodes you found yourself in and how you got yourself out of them. Or, you can tell them about times that you weren't resourceful and ask how they would have fixed the mess.

All your teen's decisions may not be good ones, no matter how much you practice or present cases. If your teen is struggling with a situation, have them draw a line down the center of a piece of paper. On one side, they list the problem and on the other, they brainstorm and list the solutions. Then, have them rank the solutions numerically, best to worst. Furthermore, after describing something your teen encountered, have them rank how they solved the problem on a scale of one to five, with five being the best. Be consistent in having them use the rating scale when resolving problems, and give feedback and encouragement for a job well done.

Here are some ways to increase your teen's resourcefulness quotient:

- Teach them to change a tire, jump-start a car, and who to call after a car accident.

- Show how to tip servers at a restaurant.

- Make sure they know how to find and call a taxi or look up bus schedules.

- Demonstrate or discuss how to apply for a job and how to keep it.

Build Traditions

Traditions define who you are as a family and connect your past to your present. They are the special ways your family celebrates life, holidays, and turning points. You gain strength as a family with each tradition as clear memories of irreplaceable sounds, smells, and tastes link one generation to the next.

You may not even realize you have established these customs until you try to do something different! The warm smell of gingerbread baking announces that the holidays are near for one family. The scent lingers throughout the house as dozens of gingerbread men are baked and decorated. Another family takes "first photographs" and hangs them on a wall with all the other pictures of family "firsts."

Wrap your family in a blanket of security by building your traditions.

Place a candle in the window. Family members far from home know you're awaiting their safe return.

Make a fire. Light a fire on cold winter nights to create warmth, security, and a refuge in a storm.

Tie a yellow ribbon. Welcome returning family members after they have been away a long time.

Birthdays. Make the whole day special. Place a sign in the school yard, bake a favorite cake, wash your teen's car, or tape an "I'm so glad you were born" note on their mirror.

Valentine's Day. Bake heart-shaped sugar cookies or red velvet cake. Add red food coloring to each side dish at dinner, or sprinkle red Jell-O powder onto the snow in the shape of a heart.

Easter. Fill small plastic eggs with redeemable coupons or quarters and hide them. Play an egg-toss game or decorate boiled eggs with sequins or ribbons. Sprinkle flour around the front door to make rabbit paw prints or fill Easter baskets and send them to kids in college.

Graduation. Create a memory board with pictures of your teen from infancy to graduation or watch home videos from birth through high school. Write a personal graduation letter or fill a container for college with a miniature tool set and sewing and medicine kits.

Fourth of July. Go to a local parade and afterward have a picnic complete with fried chicken, potato salad, and coleslaw. Later, lay on blankets watching fireworks burst in brilliant configurations. "Ooh! and aah! in appreciation.

Thanksgiving. At dinner, have each person express what they are thankful for. Roll leftover pie crust into pinwheels of butter and cinnamon. Put one Indian corn on a rope for each family member and nail it to front door, or play football in the front yard.

Christmas. Play Christmas music while decorating or have a special dedecorating day. Fill stockings with unusual gifts, set up a holiday jigsaw puzzle, or make wreaths out of boughs cut from your tree. Bake and decorate a gingerbread house.

New Year's Eve. Create a special meal to be eaten at 11 P.M. Have hats and blowers for midnight, or watch the ball come down at midnight on TV.

Once upon a Time: Become the Family Gatekeeper

Since a very early age, Kaity had heard countless stories of the generations of strong women of her family. They survived hurricanes, wars, and the loss of babies and loved ones. In all cases, each and every woman triumphed over adversity. And every time they fell down, they would pick themselves up and go forward, better than before. Kaity grew up knowing with an unwavering certainty that she, too, was strong and part of a great legacy of women who not only survived, but thrived.

Your teen is a patchwork of memories, traditions, and family history, bonded together through love, forgiveness, legend, and truth. To become the gatekeeper, the historian and glue, you must first choose a positive family theme. Common family themes are "Triumph over Adversity," "Persevere When Challenged," and "Blessed Be the Giver" (someone who has everything, but makes life better for others). Whatever theme you choose, apply it to your own family history. Even in the most dysfunctional families, you can find positive actions that will demonstrate your theme. Storytelling is a nonthreatening way to instill the values of the people your teen knows or has heard stories about over the years. Quickly, these sagas will be integrated into their own personal history, so ancestors become blended into their past and future.

Be the troubadour, the magi, and the teller of tales. Start early and weave these stories of strength, compassion, wisdom, and kindness into their experience. Let the roots seek deep soil and be nourished by those they came from, to help your teen become who they will be.

Everyone needs a hero or heroine. Find one or more in your own family and tell your teen how they resemble the family's heroes by connecting similarities between them. These similarities can include your teen's ambition, humor, or the way they work through problems. Build a legend of success to help your teen discover to whom they are forever linked and the hero in themselves.

Go through your old photos and create a visual legend. Make a separate album with little captions under each picture, lovingly placed in chronological order. Point out the sequence of your teen's life, and who has been involved in it over time. Your teen will be caught up in the stories as you show them the great heritage of their family. Explore your ancestry and create a family tree to arouse curiosity. Take your teen on a trip to see the home you grew up in or the meadows where you played. Learning about these achievements and perils will connect them forever to their family and generate a feeling of belonging.

Tell your teen about the faces that they are looking at. One teenage daughter was taking business courses in college and decided to transfer to the psychology program. She told her father, "I don't know why, but I just feel like I need to be in a career that helps others who are less fortunate." Her father was in the business world himself and spent considerable time showing her how she could help people through this field. Despite her father's reassurance, the years of listening to stories of family members who had fought in wars, worked in orphanages, and doctored the ill in poverty-stricken areas created a compelling need for this teen to continue the tradition.

Your family is the framework of your teen's life. This legacy will teach them to give back to someone else in the family. When you choose to give birth, you also choose to develop a human soul who adds to the life you gave them. You want to develop your teen into a productive, responsible member of the family. They will learn through your teachings and discover the great joy of knowing why they are here.

There's No Place Like Home

Stephen's lower lip trembled as he said good-bye to his mother before entering his first-grade classroom. His mother smiled with compassion, bent down, and placed a lipstick kiss onto the palm of his hand. Closing his fingers she said, "Whenever you are afraid Stephen, open your palm and know I am with you." Twelve years later, Stephen, a 6'2" teen going off to college, stooped down to give his mother a hug. Wrapping her in his arms, Stephen's mother could feel his body trembling. Just as before, his mother softly took her son's large hand in hers, opened his palm and placed a gentle kiss. Smiling up with tears in her eyes, she whispered, "Stephen, I am always with you."

In our mobile society, you may have lived in many houses, but you are the "home," and you take it wherever you go. Your home is a refuge your teen can return to when they need comfort, love, and acceptance. You are and always will be the number one influence in your teen's life. They feel safe at home, tucked in with memories of celebration and appreciation. Even though they may be pushing for more independence, they are still scared and unsure of what lies ahead.

Your teen needs your love and attention just as much as they did when they were young. You provide the safety net when they mess up or feel low. Through your dedication and commitment to bring love, peace, and harmony into your home, you have given your teen a safe place to be themselves without boasting or pretense. Your family is the one group your teen knows with absolute certainty that they belong to.

As much as they push back, your teen finds comfort in the standards you've set and the rituals you've established. They feel secure, knowing their birthdays will be celebrated, their holidays joyful, and their well-being the highest priority. Your teen knows when their behaviors will be appreciated and which ones will be challenged. They have no doubt their room awaits them when they've been gone and that your arms will hold them when they are sad. And they have discovered through your years of understanding and care that not all their days will be good, but tomorrow will be better.

In your home, they've been well taught to ask for what they need and how to give without expecting anything in return. They have learned to look at mistakes as learning experiences and to not only get up, but also try again. Perseverance has become a virtue and integrity their greatest attribute. Through your constant advocacy, your teen believes anything is possible if they set their mind to it, and that character is more than just one act of kindness.

You have created a home of compassion, courage, and hope. To connect with your teen you have worked hard at understanding how you could be the best parent possible. Regardless of the challenges, you face these adolescent years with the belief that by decorating your home with love and laughter, it can become your teen's touchstone when they need tranquillity before greeting the world.

Some Other New Harbinger Titles

Helping Your Depressed Child, Item 3228 $14.95

The Couples's Guide to Love and Money, Item 3112 $18.95

50 Wonderful Ways to be a Single-Parent Family, Item 3082 $12.95

Caring for Your Grieving Child, Item 3066 $14.95

Helping Your Child Overcome an Eating Disorder, Item 3104 $16.95

Helping Your Angry Child, Item 3120 $17.95

The Stepparent's Survival Guide, Item 3058 $17.95

Drugs and Your Kid, Item 3015 $15.95

The Daughter-In-Law's Survival Guide, Item 2817 $12.95

Whose Life Is It Anyway?, Item 2892 $14.95

It Happened to Me, Item 2795 $17.95

Act it Out, Item 2906 $19.95

Parenting Your Older Adopted Child, Item 2841 $16.95

Boy Talk, Item 271X $14.95

Talking to Alzheimer's, Item 2701 $12.95

Helping a Child with Nonverbal Learning Disorder or Asperger's Syndrome, Item 2779 $14.95

The 50 Best Ways to Simplify Your Life, Item 2558 $11.95

When Anger Hurts Your Relationship, Item 2604 $13.95

The Couple's Survival Workbook, Item 254X $18.95

Loving Your Teenage Daughter, Item 2620 $14.95

Call **toll free, 1-800-748-6273,** or log on to our online bookstore at **www.newharbinger.com** to order. Have your Visa or Mastercard number ready. Or send a check for the titles you want to New Harbinger Publications, Inc., 5674 Shattuck Ave., Oakland, CA 94609. Include $4.50 for the first book and 75¢ for each additional book, to cover shipping and handling. (California residents please include appropriate sales tax.) Allow two to five weeks for delivery.

Prices subject to change without notice.